SIX SECONDS TO
TRUE CALM™

THRIVING SKILLS FOR 21ST CENTURY LIVING

SIX SECONDS TO

TRUE CALM™

By

ROBERT SIMON SIEGEL, M.S.

Little Sun Books

Publisher's Cataloging-in-Publication Data

Siegel, Robert Simon.
    Six seconds to True Calm : thriving skills for 21st century living / by Robert Simon Siegel.
    p. cm.
    Includes bibliographical references.
    Preassigned LCCN: 95-95070
    ISBN 0-9648702-0-7
    1. Health   2. Self-care, Health.   3. Stress management.
    4. Psychology, Applied .   I. Title

RA776.S54 1995   613
                  QBI95-20591

Cover design and art direction by Clifford Sam.
Original cover art by Ira Ono.

ISBN 0-9648702-0-7

Library of Congress Catalog Card Number 95-95070

This book is manufactured in the United States of America.
1 2 3 4 5 6 7 8 9

Published by Little Sun Books, P.O. Box 952, Santa Monica, CA 90406.

DEDICATION

Jonathan

For your wisdom, humor and loving guidance along the path of energy

&

Johnnie Cordell Breed

For your brilliance, your heart and the wonder of our friendship

TABLE OF CONTENTS

PREFACE

W|e are a "stressed out" society. Increasingly that phrase "stressed out" enters our everyday conversations. We accept the discomforts and symptoms of stress as normal - the unavoidable cost of living in today's demanding environment. Nearly everyone feels the daily toll of stress in the form of headaches, upset stomachs, tense muscles, racing thoughts, insomnia, fatigue, worry, anxiety, emotional upset and more.

Why hasn't science yet found a cure for stress?

Many scientists, researchers and health care professionals believe that stress can cause, worsen and prevent the healing of a huge range of health problems - physical, mental and emotional. The actual mechanisms by which stress harms, they feel, are clearly established in conditions of hypertension, heart disease, ulcers, heart attacks, immune function, diabetes and possibly some forms of cancer.

Yet, despite an abundance of such research, other scientists, researchers and physicians remain unconvinced that stress influences health, or that there is even such a thing as "stress."

A third group of scientists and researchers state the necessity to recognize stress as a unique phenomenon which requires unique criteria for proper evaluation. In fact, we remain without an accepted and precise definition of stress.

Still, practicing physicians and psychotherapists verify that most of their caseload is due to stress. The American Institute of Stress states that 75% - 90% of all doctor visits are stress-related.

A primary reason that a remedy has not yet been found for our unhealthy response to life's inevitable stresses is that scientific research tends to focus on describing the body's symptoms of stress as "problems," rather than as potentially **beneficial messages.** In addition, mainstream science has failed to perceive these "stress signals" as a small part of a larger process.

Not a random event, stress has enormous evolutionary purpose, but we have been misinterpreting its positive function. Stress is actually part of our intuition. It talks to us through our body as pure intuition, serving to guide us benevolently through change. To make our symptoms of stress go away, we simply need to get their valuable message. In this light, taking pills, drugs and alcohol to numb the messages is a great disservice to ourselves.

But how do we tune in when the frenzied discomforts of stress are rattling our mind, body and emotions? We instantly **activate** our innate calming mechanism, the ancient mind/body state already built into our physiology: **TRUE CALM.** Simply by operating four of our body systems together in a certain manner all at the same time we can improve our health, dissolve all forms of stress, and mechanically feel calm - within six seconds - whenever we want!

Note to Readers:

The quotes from the works of Idries Shah are taken out of the context of his writings and are herein used for my specific purposes, which are of a far more narrow scope than his. For a proper and more complete understanding of his extraordinary material, readers are encouraged to experience his writings directly.

This book is intended as an educational tool. The methods described in this book should not be substituted for the advice and treatment of a licensed health professional, but rather should be used in conjunction with professional care when appropriate.

ACKNOWLEDGMENTS

*F*irst of all, I want to thank John Maragioglio for being my great friend and partner in an extraordinary growth process. May the adventures continue forever. Again I must thank Johnnie Cordell Breed for her inspiration, insistence, support and dedication to this project. Without you, it may never have happened. Ira Ono for bringing the Big Island spirit and the spices of your everwondrous art over the years. To Pete Sotos for your friendship and constant genius in fixing everything from cars and computers to business deals. My gratitude to Maryalice O'Hearn for all you shared.

Many special people comprised my book team. I thank you all for guiding me through this project with grace, integrity and encouragement. Susan Heyer did a marvelous job as editor of nearly all of the manuscript. Thank you for putting the shine on my work and for keeping it true to my style of communication. Art Director Clifford Sam produced the stunning graphics throughout the book and the inspired cover design. I greatly appreciate your beyond-the-call efforts to meet deadlines and think ahead. You delivered the goods! To Gene Church, Project Coordinator, I thank you for your constant good cheer, humor and encouragement, and for focusing me on each next step with joy for an approaching accomplishment. Thanks to Mary Ivory for your enthusiasm and for connecting me with Gene.

To my illustrator, John Lusarreta, I thank you for your patience, your ability to visually portray my concepts, and your steadfast willingness to make it right. It was a pleasure working with you. Jim Strohecher and Nancy Shaw, thank you for your considerable energy, which came at the right time to guide me through the details of completion and what comes next. Your unique understanding of my project provided the perspective, the confirmation and confidence I needed for stepping out.

My thanks to Robin Quinn for a truly impressive job at copy editing. You made a believer out of me! Laura Bellotti, you wrote inspired cover copy with remarkable speed. Thanks for your cogent understanding of my book and for your mastery of your craft. Thanks to Rohit Chitale for helping with research.

I want to thank Cleaves Bennett, M.D. for the opportunity to work with you in treating hypertensive patients and for your encouragement to write the book. Chris Sherman and Al Van Lund from Pacific Enterprises, I am grateful for your belief in my program as a benefit for corporations and for your actions that made it happen. To Dr. Elmer Green, I am grateful for your valuable and timely input.

To the many clients who actively applied these skills into their daily lives, your feedback was essential in refining my understanding. Thank you for your challenges to make **TRUE CALM** practical and relevant. Special thanks to Lorraine Tiffany-Malone at the Pritikin Longevity Center for your support.

Finally, to my friends and family members who kept their faith in me throughout years of struggle, I love you all.

···INTRODUCTION···

"There is no such thing as a problem without a gift for you in its hands. We attract the problem because we seek the gift." [1]

I was running across campus at the College of William and Mary to deliver an oral presentation to my Educational Psychology class. No big deal. I had experience with public speaking, comfortable since grade school giving speeches to PTA assemblies and student bodies, as well as playing music and sports in front of crowds. What an easy choice: to slave over a written term paper, or talk for one hour? No contest.

Having been on the cross-country team in high school, jogging the six blocks to class was effortless. As I dashed into the building, the teacher saw me coming and introduced me to the class. As a result, when I entered the classroom, I was "on." I had practiced my delivery earlier, making a dramatic case for the topic of "How Children Fail." In my presentation I planned to remind my audience of how it feels when the teacher calls on YOU to answer a tough question, and all of the other students turn and focus their attention on you. Now all eyes were staring at me.

What happened next would change my entire life. It had never occurred to me that I might need to catch my breath before speaking. Instead of a smooth, focused delivery I uttered but two words before the heaving of my chest overpowered my attempts to speak. One hundred students - friends, peers and col-leagues - were staring at me in amusement while I gasped for air, wondering if I was dying. Out of control and totally unable to form words, not knowing what in the world was going on while being the center of everyone's attention, I generated my first full-fledged panic attack!

All I wanted to do was run out of the room screaming. Fortunately, someone asked me to start over since they couldn't hear me, and I managed to catch my breath enough to speak - very humbly and with knees shaking! For the next twelve years even the thought of public speaking immediately made my heart pound, my adrenaline rush and my muscles tense. I would get dizzy and light-headed. My thoughts would scatter and I couldn't remember anything I wanted to say. This was not joyous stress. Major fear of public speaking had set in. It quickly generalized to every area of my life, so that even casual and friendly situations involving two or more people would trigger panic attacks. Then it began to occur when I was talking to a single person. It became very hard to be cool, calm and collected.

In graduate school I somehow became attracted to, fully fascinated with, the newly emerging phenomenon of STRESS. Like a powerful magnet, stress seized my attention. I was not alone. In fact, a new field of science, behavioral medicine, came into being to address stress, which was cutting across the boundaries of standard disciplines. It didn't quite fit into physical medicine, because it clear-ly involved mental and emotional behaviors. Nor did it fully fit into psychology, because a vast array of physical symptoms were evident. I thought it most amusing that physicians now had to admit that humans had a mind, and that the mind definitely affects our body. Psychologists, on the other hand, were forced to accept that the body affects our emotions and our mental activity. So... they needed to talk.

As a result of my graduate research and specialization, I began getting professional speaking engagements as an "expert" on stress. It was like a cosmic joke - but on me! "You folks want to see stress?" I would think. "No problem. Just watch me freak out and run from the room screaming!"

After too many years during which my life and income were squelched by having to refuse any situation with the potential for speaking in front of a group of people, I realized that in order to have some integrity I needed to conquer my anxiety. I researched in earnest every relaxation and stress "management" technique in the books. Living on the East Coast, I hunted for clinicians in New York, Boston, Connecticut. Wherever there was someone who knew anything about relieving stress, I was there.

Nothing worked for me.

Not being a physician who could prescribe medications for relief, I was forced to analyze every mind, body and emotional system involved in panic attacks, anxiety, nervousness and stress with the goal of gaining self control - without pills, drugs or alcohol. Over time, using biofeedback medical scanning equipment and working with thousands of folks who were suffering with a wide range of stress conditions in many settings - hospitals, preventive medicine centers, wellness centers, psychiatric clinics, public seminars and corporations - I found answers.

First I found there were four main body systems involved. While stress programs typically gave tools for handling one or maybe two of these systems, all four were necessary in order to gain the solid confidence that comes only with proven success under pressure. I found that one could indeed gain control over these four systems in precise ways using "body/mind control levers." And I discovered that these levers can be operated by focusing one's attention in certain ways.

I found that the people who were successful in remedying their stress, panic and anxiety accomplished similar things. They learned to focus their attention in these specific ways, and they recognized the existence of a deeper, more mysterious element. They came to understand and trust that their so-called "stress" was no random event, but that it had valuable meaning and important purpose. They "got" that their stress serves as a sort of communication device, like an intuitive sixth sense, guiding them quite benevolently. These fortunate folks experienced time and again that when they received its message and acted on it with respect, they experienced often profound personal growth, their lives improved, AND...

the stress went away - naturally!

In fact, I now consider "stress" to be the unhealthy result of ineffective, destructive reactions to our intuition. By responding positively to our communication system, we benefit and thrive. This book is about how to thrive. The gifts my own stress has produced are immense. I now **LOVE** speaking to groups and have great fun doing so. Best of all is making contact with this wondrous inner part that communicates through "stress." Knowing you have a wiser aspect to yourself that has your very best interests at heart adds an enormously rich dimension to daily life. This inner part **IS** you, the **REAL** you, and is guiding you most benevolently, helping you fulfill your needs and desires - often with incredible humor. In time I discovered that this inner part is also the source of our creativity, our solutions, our intuition and our inner guidance.

Our next evolutionary step as human beings is to establish direct contact. How? Like tuning the radio dial to clearly receive an exceptional station, we gain access to our inner wisdom by focusing our attention in precise ways. Coincidentally, these are exactly the same ways that relieve stress by giving us lifelong control over the four main body systems involved in stress, anxiety, nervousness and panic reactions. Additionally, when we operate these systems in a more healthy manner, we accomplish more than just dissolving stress. We experience health gains so valuable that I call them *"The Four Treasured Qualities"*. They are:

Emotional Peace	*Physical Relaxation*
Presence of Mind	*Uplifting Energy*

Just as the whole is greater than the sum of its parts, when we operate these four systems in a certain fashion all at the same time, we activate a very special and health-enhancing state of "being," an ancient calming mechanism already built into our physiology. This is the human experience, deemed priceless throughout the ages, which has often been called "peace of mind."

With these mechanical skills, we can feel good inside whenever we want - anytime, anyplace - and we can do so within six seconds. To all readers, and especially to those with a more technical background, you will notice that my use of words differs from the standard scientific approach. I do this to better convey the way I have found things to be. And, if you stay with the process, you will find that it works. It is with great joy that I can now present the long-awaited natural remedy for unhealthy stress...

TRUE CALM

CHAPTER ONE

THE QUEST FOR TRUE CALM

*"Aim for knowledge. If you become poor, it will be wealth for you.
If you become rich, it will adorn you."[1]*

An increasing amount of scientific research confirms what humans have instinctively known for millennia. We have available to us a very special "state" of being, a uniquely healthy balance of body, mind, emotions and spirit which allows us to feel complete, confident, serene and whole. That we feel almost constantly separated from and deprived of this state of being is the source of much human longing. A widespread, incompletely articulated sense of frustration, pain and loss sends millions into psychotherapy or scurrying for prescription drugs to salve those feelings.

Behind these and dozens of other human behaviors is a sense that we are not fully present, not fully confident in ourselves, that we are under threat from enemies named and unnamed, and that, in the deepest sense, we are missing something. Somewhere inside, we believe...

***

THERE'S A BETTER WAY TO "BE"

And we're right. This special state of being has been called many names: bliss, peace of mind, the alpha state, heightened awareness and "being centered." It's no accident that thoughtful people throughout the ages have valued this experience as priceless. Its immediate impact alone makes it highly desirable, for in its fullest expression we have a sublime feeling of well-being that refreshes our minds, soothes our emotions, relaxes our bodies and uplifts our spirits.

Just as the term "true north" speaks of the purest measure of a geographical direction, **TRUE CALM** aptly describes this special state of being. There is magic in **TRUE CALM**. It expands our awareness, increases our creativity, enhances our intuition, and develops our understanding in ways which are sometimes described as "psychic." Being in a state of **TRUE CALM** naturally cultivates perceptual skills that no amount of scientific, analytic or intellectual education can teach. We gain the wisdom to "see the big picture." We begin to perceive how seemingly isolated events actually operate as parts of a larger whole.

Tasting **TRUE CALM** inspires us to want more, like a sweet, juicy mouthful of your favorite fruit. The pleasures of **TRUE CALM** attract, seducing us again and again by making us feel so good inside. Its smooth ride satisfies our senses like a slow massage.

Unique things happen to us in a state of **TRUE CALM**. We feel a clear boost in our energy. Our aging processes slow, our body's self-healing systems work with greater speed and efficiency, and our immune system is stimulated. Our muscles release, improving our circulation.[2] Our heartbeat slows[3] and our blood pressure lowers.[4] Our mind clears[5] and our brain's right and left cortex work together as a whole. Our brain waves become slower, smoother and more regular. Overall, we simply feel good. We're happier more and more of the time.

A great many medications are prescribed to imitate the qualities of **TRUE CALM**, often with dangerous physical and psychological side effects. We might abuse alcohol and illegal drugs to capture a simulated taste of the euphoria and relief **TRUE CALM** offers. We try in vain to gain calm by purchasing costly health and insurance plans to cover frightening eventualities reported daily through the media's unsettling news. We may travel to exotic locales, subscribe to outdated spiritual systems, follow gurus and embrace bizarre programs, relationships, or rituals, going to great expense and extraordinary lengths to experience the benefits of **TRUE CALM**.

Yet the ability to achieve that coveted state of being is easily within our grasp, at no material cost. And it has been all along. The following fable is from a collection of Sufi stories featuring the lovable folklore character, Mulla Nasrudin, who often illustrates truth by playing the fool. It suggests how people throughout the ages have sought this knowledge in "all the wrong places."

There Is More Light Here

Someone saw Nasrudin searching for something on the ground.

"What have you lost, Mulla?" he asked.
"My key," said the Mulla.

So they both went down on their knees and looked for it. After a time the other man asked:

"Where exactly did you drop it?"
"In my house."
"Then why are you looking here?"

Mulla Nasrudin replied: "There is more light here than inside my own house."

The Exploits of the Incomparable Mulla Nasrudin, Idries Shah,
The Octagon Press, London, 1966.

It often seems quicker or easier to achieve calm, self-control and inner peace by reaching for a magic pill, a drink, drugs, or for someone or something to blame, as if there were more "light" outside ourselves. That's the familiar "external" approach. But Nasrudin's silliness points to truth. The "key" to **TRUE CALM**, to our happiness and well-being, is actually inside ourselves.

For most people, including physicians and psychologists, health is a concept which in practice is limited to the absence of illness, stress, pain, discomfort and problems. But genuine health goes beyond merely reducing, managing and eliminating health problems. Real health is about feeling great, much better than just "ok" or "not bad." Real wellness is about feeling fully alive, increasingly aware, invigorated with mental clarity and confidence, actively enjoying progress toward our goals and desires.

The positive feelings we seek through tranquilizers, alcohol and other drugs can be produced without external agents.

You can achieve those feelings independently and whenever you wish. With **TRUE CALM,** the cost to your bank account, your health and your self-esteem is nil. It is easy and natural because...

TRUE CALM is already built into our physiology.

We simply need to learn how to turn it on. The side effects are increased self-confidence, greater health and the ability to feel good inside whenever you choose.

You can achieve **TRUE CALM** through mechanical exercises that turn on...

***

The Four Treasured Qualities

The cornerstones of **TRUE CALM** are also the qualities cultivated and possessed by happy, healthy, successful, creative people. These foundations for physical, mental and emotional wellness, for contentment and confidence, and for an expansive embrace of life itself are:

> *Emotional Peace*
> *Physical Relaxation*
> *Presence of Mind*
> *Uplifting Energy*

I call these attributes *The Four Treasured Qualities* (fig. 1.1)

The
Four Treasured Qualities
of

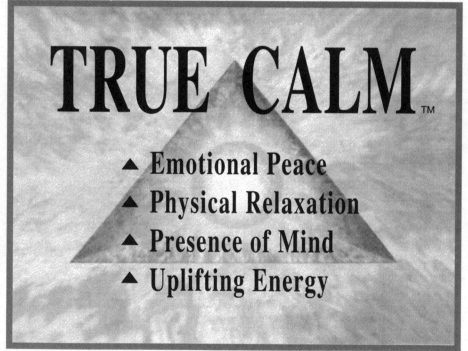

Fig. 1.1

The Four Treasured Qualities refer to four different body systems. By mechanically activating each body system in a specific and healthy fashion, we can easily gain *The Four Treasured Qualities.* Each naturally produces an array of wonderful health benefits. Correspondingly, when these four body systems are operating in an unhealthy and ineffective manner, they mechanically produce <u>all</u> forms of stress - physical, mental, emotional and spiritual. As we gain control, each separate system relieves a specific category of stress, thus remedying and preventing its accompanying category of health problems. Figure 1.2 shows the range of both health benefits and health problems connected with each body system.

The secret is to operate all four systems in concert with each other. This is key. Sometimes people can get one system going, perhaps even two systems. That's good! However, operating the four together is necessary to achieve the vast benefits of this ancient calming mechanism. The genuine state of **TRUE CALM** is a whole much greater than the sum of its parts. This is why we can say with confidence:

TRUE CALM
is the long-awaited natural remedy for destructive stress!

Throughout this book we will explore simple but unusually effective ways to accomplish **TRUE CALM** by building each of *The Four Treasured Qualities*. Let's examine their unique benefits.

THE FOUR TREASURED QUALITIES OF TRUE CALM

HEALTHY FUNCTIONING

EMOTIONAL PEACE
Feeling Centered and Secure

Emotions of Happiness and Joy

Refreshed Moods

Clearer Perspective on What's Important to You

Feeling More Comfortable Inside Yourself

Autonomic Nervous System

PHYSICAL RELAXATION
Improved Circulation of Blood, Oxygen and Lymph Fluids

Pleasures of Deep Relaxation

Dissolving Headaches Quickly

Soothing Relief of Tension

Pleasures of Letting Go

Skeletal Muscle System

PRESENCE OF MIND
Sharper Mental Clarity

Greater Sensory Awareness

Stronger Concentration

Increased Creativity and Intuition

Confident Focus Under Pressure

Living More in the Present

Central Nervous System

UPLIFTING ENERGY
Increased Aliveness

Recharged Immune System

Invigorating, Soothing Energy

Elevating Self-Esteem

Rejuvenated Spirits

Feeling the Nourishing Energy that We Call Love and Joy

Life Energy System

UNHEALTHY FUNCTIONING

- *High Blood Pressure*
- *Upset Stomach*
- *Rapid Heartbeat*
- *Depression*
- *Emotional Upset*
- *Anger*
- *Frustration*
- *Fear*
- *Ulcers*

- *Neck/Shoulder Pain*
- *Stomach Knots*
- *Shortness of Breath*
- *Stiff Joints*
- *Muscular Tension*
- *Headaches*
- *Chest Tightness*

- *Too Many Thoughts at Once*
- *Nervousness*
- *Poor Concentration*
- *Insomnia*
- *Racing Thoughts*
- *Insecurity*
- *Panic Attacks*
- *Worry*
- *Anxiety*

- *Over-Taxed Adrenals*
- *Low Self-Esteem*
- *Immune Weakness*
- *Rapid Aging*
- *Poor Confidence*
- *Fatigue*

Fig. 1.2

Emotional Peace - Treasured Quality #1

How do we assign a value to feeling great inside? How much is it worth to be emotionally serene, to enjoy freedom from life's emotional turmoil, to be rejuvenated by a feeling of inner peace? When our emotions are calm, our quality of life - our attitudes, relationships, confidence and self-esteem - all change for the better. We regain perspective on life, and on what's important to us. We become clearer about what we really want to do with our time and energy.

When we have inner peace, the more positive emotions of happiness, security and contentment seem to bubble up effortlessly. Our capacity to feel love, to offer and receive love, grows. On a deeper level, a special type of happiness emerges, an inner joy which touches our very souls. We feel at one with ourselves, with others, and with life.

You will learn to put into place the physiological foundation for *Emotional Peace* in part through two unique and quite simple respiratory maneuvers - by breathing.

Physical Relaxation - Treasured Quality #2

When we speak of relaxing, we actually refer to the physical release of muscle tension. Like a soothing massage, *Physical Relaxation* is a sensual delight, and it is much more than idle luxury. *Physical Relaxation* is a health necessity. It enhances our overall well-being, not just by eliminating the aches and pains of muscle tension, but also by increasing our cardiovascular and lymph fluid circulation, dissolving headaches, loosening our joints, relieving nerve pressures, lowering blood lactate, and reducing the workload for our heart and lungs.[6]

9

With *Physical Relaxation* we can think and concentrate better, our spirits improve, and we become more imaginative and creative. Our pleasure in life increases as our bodies operate in greater harmony with our desires and needs. Our bodies seem to take us, quite obligingly, wherever we need to go, as escorts rather than as baggage.

You will learn to achieve *Physical Relaxation* whenever you choose by guiding your skeletal muscle system's nine major muscle groups through a basic series of tension-release exercises - by <u>feeling</u>. Then you will learn to relax these muscles more quickly and deeply. Finally, you will learn how to relax your whole body <u>within six seconds</u>!

Presence of Mind - Treasured Quality #3

One of life's greatest pleasures is the increased "aliveness" we experience when our minds are clear and focused fully in the present. We exult in rich delights of greater awareness when our senses - touch, taste, smell, sight and hearing - **WAKE UP** and become involved in perceiving what's going on AS it is happening. The world itself seems fresh, more real, imbued with an animated vitality.

This expanded sensory awareness, *Presence of Mind,* improves our concentration, our capacity to learn and remember, and our ability to solve problems. It even helps us to better decide what is a truly a "problem" and what is <u>not</u>! *Presence of Mind* opens us up to increased creativity, intuitive understanding and an enhanced sense of the larger patterns of life itself. We remember more clearly because we perceive more fully when things are actually happening. Our zest for life increases along with our sense of serenity. We feel more alive because we <u>are</u>.

Like turning the radio dial to a crisp, clear FM station, you will learn to achieve *Presence of Mind* through <u>focusing your attention</u> in certain simple ways.

Uplifting Energy - Treasured Quality #4

Imagine having a faucet of invigorating, soothing energy flowing inside you, energy you can turn on at will, and which continually refreshes you. Feeling energized is like owning an inner fountain of youth. Our spirits are raised when we're energized, and the joys of existence are more evident. We see life as full of unexpected adventures, challenges we're eager to meet, fun we can have, and people we enjoy. With uplifted energy, we go beyond our expectations and accomplish great achievements.

We are more than simply physical, mental and emotional creatures. Humans are also composed of a network of energy patterns which flow through and around us like circulatory systems. The greater our flow of *Life Energy,* the healthier we are, the better our immune system functions, and the more joyous we feel. Blockages in these patterns of energy flow can cause health problems, leaving us listless, unmotivated and depressed. Improving this flow produces a wonderful, quiet high that underlies our best moods, our brightest moments and our peak experiences.

While the concept of energy fields and energy flow may be new to some of us, it has been well-known and utilized for centuries in the older, more continuous cultures of the world. We <u>do</u> have the ability to increase our life force by finding and opening this inner source of energy. This is also an act of self love that raises our confidence, self-esteem, sense of self and our personal power beyond what even years of successful psychotherapy can accomplish precisely because it directly connects us with the very source of our intuition and creativity: the inner guidance called our "CENTER," or our larger "SELF." Opening up this flow and bathing in our own life force is one of the healthiest, most profound (and sensual!) experiences we can have.

Uplifting Energy is the crown jewel of TRUE CALM.

As you will see, **TRUE CALM is not about being asleep!** Nor does it mean clamping down, shutting out, repressing, or "stuffing" our feelings. **TRUE CALM is about being more fully alive!**

You will learn to access *Uplifting Energy* through an elegantly simple, magical exercise which allows you to know yourself at a higher level - the level of pure energy.

***

A NEW MILLENNIUM AND
THE GLOBAL NEED FOR CALM

In our world of accelerating change, unending stress, and constant bombardment by noise, pollution, and sensory overload, **the ability to turn on our own state of TRUE CALM is now a daily necessity for survival.** Today we need, more than ever, our full immune strength to combat the avalanche of pollutants, toxins, chemicals, radiation and electromagnetic dangers building up in our environment. This noxious situation will be worsening before it improves because we have not halted the production of these health poisons at their sources. Surviving this affront requires maximum immune strength. **TRUE CALM** and, in particular, *Uplifting Energy*, which will be discussed later in the book, have vital roles in boosting immunity.

It is no accident we crave more calm. Calm is the foundation for vibrant good health. By conserving and recharging our energy, **TRUE CALM slows the aging process and strengthens our immunity.** **TRUE CALM** <u>remedies virtually all harmful conditions of stress</u>. It can help relieve and minimize the unhealthy effects of numerous attendant ailments, including:

headaches	fatigue
neck and back pain	nervousness
pinched nerves	poor self-esteem
high blood pressure	insomnia
hypertension	overeating
ulcers	anger
colitis	racing thoughts
arthritis	poor concentration
angina	anxiety
heart attacks	depression
strokes	fear
upset stomach	panic attacks

TRUE CALM promotes healing. In fact, doctors invoke the innate healing powers of calm every time they prescribe rest to nurture swift recovery. Physicians who value the effects of calm have often had to prescribe costly synthetic drugs to simulate its benefits, medications that generally provide only an approximation of calm, often with dangerous side effects. **TRUE CALM** generates its abundant health benefits naturally. Along with fitness and nutrition, the state of **TRUE CALM** completes the essential triangle for good health. (See Figure 1.3)

ESSENTIAL GOOD HEALTH TRIANGLE

Three behaviors which form the foundation for positive health (wellness) and illness prevention

Fig. 1.3

TRUE CALM is also a vital psychological and social tool for the twenty-first century. These next decades will be demanding. Among the challenges ahead of us are overpopulation and overcrowding, the threats of war and terrorism resulting from tribalism and territorial disputes, and the vulnerability of our increasingly fragile ecological systems. These and other unforetold conflicts will require wisdom, compassionate attitudes, and imaginative action to yield peaceful solutions.

It is certain that we need to search for new skills and attitudes to manage life - our own and the life of the planet. Our familiar ways of thinking, feeling and behaving are giving us neither the solutions nor the vision we need to guide our future. Although our intellectual understanding is advancing rapidly, we seem unable to "grow up." The behaviors, thoughts and emotions of our species seem stuck at an adolescent level of maturity.

What is preventing us from becoming the advanced, benevolent, loving, wondrously creative people we know we are capable of becoming? What is keeping us from living fully and joyfully in respectful harmony with each other and all forms of life? Basically...

We're Scared!!

We're almost always worried about something - having enough money, keeping a job, avoiding accidents, and eluding illness. We worry about future wars; we're wary of other races, other religions, other nations, the opposite sex and our neighbor down the street. We're rightly concerned about the safety of the food we eat, the air we breathe, and the water we drink. We fear fire, flood, drought, epidemics, earthquakes and the future itself. We try to put these fears out of our minds. However, they remain at the forefront of our daily thoughts, producing a background of impending doom and constant insecurity. We're stressed beyond "out." What exactly is going **on** here?

Simply put, after millennia of existence, **we're still stuck in survival**. We remain mechanically locked into the physiology, mentality, emotionality and behaviors of <u>an ancient survival response whose present day and very positive, evolutionary purpose is being lost on us</u>. **Anger and fear** remain our first and most immediate responses to change, as well as to any perceived threat, real or imagined. And the stress that results - the polar opposite of **TRUE CALM** - imperils not only our evolution, but our very survival.

Can we grow beyond our primitive stress responses of anger and fear? We must. There's no choice. And it's easy. But first let's explore some of the basics of stress, survival, and how we got where we are.

***

UNDERSTANDING STRESS

Modern stress, as it is often defined, has its roots in the ancient physiological survival mechanism called the **"fight/flight emergency response."**[7] We share this mechanism with our cave-dwelling ancestors, with animals, and even with some multi-celled organisms.

Survival is pure instinct. When we are confronted with an actual life-threatening situation, the will to live mobilizes enormous amounts of our energy to help us "pull out all the stops" so we can fight or run for our lives. Survival becomes our total focus.

Imagine being back in the cave-dwelling days, our prehistoric good old days. You're strolling through the woods, thinking about a nice gazelle steak waiting for you back at the cave. Suddenly, you get an urge to look up. There in a tree, entertaining his own choice of menu and ready to pounce on you, is a sabertoothed tiger! (Figure 1.4)

The subsequent human body response is a spectacular event, an enormously powerful reaction pattern that is with us today as pure survival instinct. The physiological changes we instantly experience through this fight/flight response combine to give us three tools for surviving life-or-death situations. They are: (Figure 1.5)

Instant Energy   Instant Focus

Instant Mobility

First, we feel adrenaline rushing through our insides, immediately turning on our <u>sympathetic nervous system's arousal action</u> with a surge of biochemical energy that shifts our heart, lungs and internal organs into overdrive. This provides us with the physical sensations of anxiety, fear or panic. Then our muscles tense, so we can fight or flee with quick mobility. To give our muscles a blast of their fuel - blood and oxygen - our heart and lungs start pumping hard. Our blood pressure rises dramatically to turbocharge this fuel out to the major muscle groups used to fight and run: chest, shoulders, back, thighs, calves, arms. Our blood flow shifts away from the stomach area, where it's been used for digestion, and rushes out to stoke those major muscles.

FIGHT/FLIGHT SURVIVAL RESPONSE

Walking through the woods, thinking about a gazelle steak waiting back at the cave

Suddenly gets an urge to look up! (Change Awareness Signal)

Fig. 1.4

Sees a saber-toothed tiger ready to pounce

The fight / flight survival response activates

Other brilliant changes occur, all designed to save our lives. Our blood clotting mechanisms increase to protect us in case we are cut during a battle and are at risk of bleeding to death. Production of our white blood cells, part of our immune system's defense against infections, increases rapidly in case we are wounded while fighting. Our blood cholesterol level increases, to be converted into a form of glucose for more energy.

Some very interesting things happen to our **attention-focusing**. When we first see the saber-toothed tiger eyeing us with that lean, hungry look, our mental activity speeds up immensely, so that we're thinking far more quickly than our regular meandering style. People often report that during emergencies it seemed as though everything was happening at a slowed down pace, as if they had all the time in the world, or were looking at a film in slow motion. In such instances, it's possible our mental activity does speed up, so everything else seems slower in comparison. It's also possible that our conscious mind, with its analytic style of operating, is overridden by the more instinctual capabilities of our "unconscious" mind, *which can perceive more data simultaneously.*

Our **attention-focusing** also instantly shifts out of its **internal focus** - thinking about the gazelle steak back at the cave - into a totally **external focus**. Even our eye muscles contract to sharpen our visual acuity, helping us identify both the physical threat to our lives and the escape route.

In an instant, we're ready to fight or flee, supercharged with energy, mobility and focus. This beautiful survival response has been responsible for the survival of our whole species from the cave-dwelling days through the present. (See Figure 1.6)

THREE BENEFICIAL FUNCTIONS OF THE FIGHT/FLIGHT SURVIVAL RESPONSE

Instant
FOCUS

Instant
ENERGY

Instant
MOBILITY

Fig. 1.5

ENERGY EXPENDITURE
FIGHT/FLIGHT SURVIVAL RESPONSE

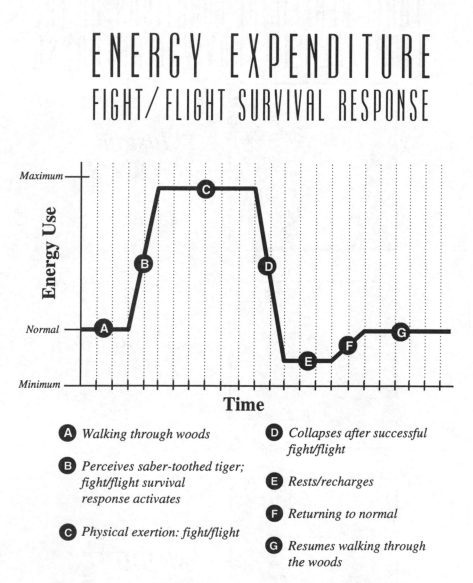

A Walking through woods

B Perceives saber-toothed tiger; fight/flight survival response activates

C Physical exertion: fight/flight

D Collapses after successful fight/flight

E Rests/recharges

F Returning to normal

G Resumes walking through the woods

The short term cycle of intensive energy use and energy regeneration during survival activities of physical fight/flight.

Fig. 1.6

In fact, many of humanity's greatest achievements have been accomplished with the help of the fight/flight emergency response's gifts of energy, mobility and focus. They help us evolve when necessity becomes "the mother of invention." We have heard tales of mothers who, upon seeing a child crawling under a parked car that has begun to roll, rushed over and hoisted up the front end of the car - then pulled the child to safety with their other hand!

How did this beautiful and wise survival mechanism go from being the protector of our species to becoming the number one contributor to heart disease, strokes, diabetes and cancer? How did it become the cause of between 75% and 90% of all doctor visits, both medical and psychological?[8] What happened?

WE CHANGED: We became more "mental."

We have evolved from being primarily physical crea- tures, using our sense organs to stay fully focused in the physical realm to hunt for our food and fight for our physical survival, into being more mental creatures. Now we use our minds for nearly everything: reading, planning, thinking, writing, computing and analyzing. Today our hunting is usually limited to finding a sale, a job, or a parking place at the supermarket, activities which some- times *seem* to require the same intensity our cave-dwelling ances- tors experienced while hunting for food.

More commonly, we find ourselves at work, ready to wrap up the day, tired and out of energy, when the boss comes in with a deadline problem that needs immediate attention. (See Figure 1.7) Somehow our fight/flight mechanism kicks on: we summon the energy, become adrenalized, get creative, and we're good for another few hours.

MODERN MENTAL STRESS

Our body reacts to mental stress with fight / flight survival response as if a tiger were physically present.

Fig. 1.7

Upon completing the project, of course, we collapse. But our fight/flight mechanism has served our needs again by providing us with energy, mobility and focus <u>now channeled through our mental activities</u>. Basically, the fight/flight survival mechanism evolved with us into the mental realm, so that...

We can now trigger fight/flight just by our thoughts, without a physical threat to our lives being present!

The resulting health problem? *We're killing ourselves with the dangerously frequent and repeated triggering of our physical fight/flight response and ...*

We don't know how to turn our survival mechanism off!

On a typical day we may go to work and find our employer coming to us with a problem that demands immediate attention. Then perhaps we recall an argument we had that morning with our spouse. We remember a large dental bill coming due, or the car that needs an overhaul. Then we think about problems the kids are having at school. <u>Each</u> of those thoughts triggers a fight/flight response. And we think each thought repeatedly, maybe twice <u>each</u> per hour for say, four hours. That's a lot of fight/flight with <u>no</u> release - a huge energy drain.

Then we perform an amazing feat: we <u>adapt</u>. We push that collection of worries to the back of our minds so we can focus on getting our work accomplished. That requires even more energy output, adding to the wear and tear on our organs and immune system. That night we go home and <u>maybe</u> we go to sleep and recuperate. More likely, we toss and turn because our minds won't stop: <u>insomnia</u>. The next day our energy reserves are gone; we're irritable, frazzled and stressed. This cycle can continue for days, weeks and months without relief. (See Figure 1.8) **The buildup over time of unresolved survival reactions is the largest single health danger of modern stress.**

Designed for all-out, last-ditch, life or death crises, the fight/flight response evolved for immediate use in short-term <u>physical</u> struggles. It uses an enormous amount of our energy in the form of our body's stored vitamins, minerals, nutrients and glucose. In addition, the physiological results of the flight/fight response, which subsided or were "burned off" by the much more physically demanding lifestyles of our ancestors, now linger in our bodies without amelioration. The caveman walked two or three miles back to his cave carrying firewood after his lively encounter with the saber-toothed tiger. That exercise regulated his heart and breathing rates, returned his blood circulation and cholesterol levels to normal, and relaxed his tense muscles through movement. In contrast, we tend to return to our desks and... simply sit down.

Without the release of intense physical activity, our inner organs remain revved up, our cholesterol is raised[9] but not converted into energy, our muscles remain tensed, and our minds continue to focus on our problems, worries and insecurities. Our inner organs are "stewing" because we don't know how to turn the fight/flight reaction off. This huge energy drain taxes our immune system. The toll is rapid aging, internal organ deterioration and emotional problems.

Is it surprising that high blood pressure, ulcers, strokes, cancers, headaches, insomnia, anxiety attacks, depression and problems of immune weakness are now "normal" experiences in our daily life?

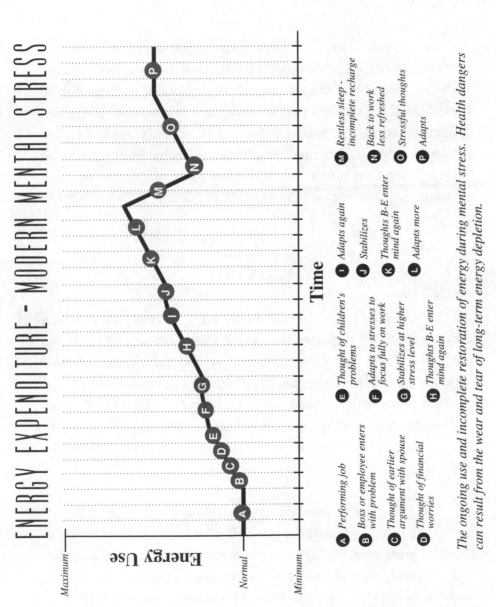

ENERGY EXPENDITURE - MODERN MENTAL STRESS

Energy Use

Maximum
Normal
Minimum

Time

- **A** Performing job
- **B** Boss or employee enters with problem
- **C** Thought of earlier argument with spouse
- **D** Thought of financial worries
- **E** Thought of children's problems
- **F** Adapts to stresses to focus fully on work
- **G** Stabilizes at higher stress level
- **H** Thoughts B-E enter mind again
- **I** Adapts again
- **J** Stabilizes
- **K** Thoughts B-E enter mind again
- **L** Adapts more
- **M** Restless sleep - incomplete recharge
- **N** Back to work less refreshed
- **O** Stressful thoughts
- **P** Adapts

The ongoing use and incomplete restoration of energy during mental stress. Health dangers can result from the wear and tear of long-term energy depletion.

Fig. 1.8

While regular exercise and proper nutrition help greatly to counter these deleterious effects of stress, they are by themselves not enough. Is there a direct solution to this absurdly problematic situation?

Just as we "conquered" the physical realm enough to navigate out of the constant quest for survival, we now need to navigate the mental and emotional realms - certainly well enough to leave behind the patterns that keep us stuck in a survival mentality. In fact, as individuals and as a species, we urgently need to evolve beyond the physical, mental, emotional and behavioral patterns of survival. It is time for us - as individuals and as a species - to move forward with purpose into the patterns of human...

***

THRIVING

THRIVING **is our birthright.** *THRIVING* **means** accomplishing as a species the very highest qualities of living on planet EARTH: our most cherished shared values, our greatest joys, our most benevolent creations, vibrant good health for all life, pristine purity of air, water, soil and food. *THRIVING* goes beyond forever battling to merely survive life, always trying to reduce, manage, prevent or even eliminate those conditions we don't want.

We have moved through our slow, painstaking development in the physical, material plane of survival, and are now on the brink of great breakthroughs in the mental realms of human experience. The irony and beauty of this next step in evolution is that in order to ensure our continued survival, **we must learn to THRIVE.**

As mental creatures, we can see how our biological heritage on a dangerous material plane has conditioned us to respond to CHANGE - that is, anything new, different, or unexpected - with fight/flight, as if CHANGE were *always* a threat to our survival. It is not. Once we are free of the oppressive limitations of our automatic survival reaction, change is our friend. Change is a marvelous vehicle for finally fulfilling our grand human potential.

Given the currently brisk rate of global change and the many challenges we're facing, we're going to have to be quick on our feet. We must...

Change our response to change itself.

Naturally, we need some very practical tools to accomplish this monumental SHIFT from being stuck grinding our gears with the stress of unhealthy, ineffective responses to change. We need to instantly stop our automatic fight/flight survival reactions from locking us into the physical, mental, emotional and behavioral patterns of **surviving** so that we can activate the physical, mental, emotional and behavioral patterns of *Thriving*. How can we do this?

First we apply a skill that uses *The Four Treasured Qualities* to mechanically turn on our body's ancient calming mechanism, the state of **TRUE CALM**, within six seconds. This eminently practical skill is...

***

instant calm

Yes, it is absolutely possible to turn on our body's ancient calming mechanism, our parasympathetic nervous system, <u>within six seconds</u>. After mastering the simple, mechanical exercises in this book, you will be able to synthesize and use them in a short-form version, whenever and wherever you wish. *Instant calm* is a fast, safe, health-enhancing skill that will serve you for a lifetime.

Secondly, we combine *instant calm* with the **attention-focusing** patterns of healthy, happy, creative, successful people to:

Respond *POSITIVELY* to change.

We apply...

***

THE THRIVING RESPONSE

The THRIVING Response is an easy, three-step method of using the state of **TRUE CALM** to respond in healthy, more effective ways to CHANGE. Throughout human history, for a variety of reasons, knowledge of how to gain the special state of **TRUE CALM** was often kept secret. People in search of its treasures often had to travel great distances to find a living master who would instruct them. Arduous tests of sincerity and great sacrifices could be required for acceptance into the teaching. The good news is that today...

YOU DON'T HAVE TO GO TO TIBET!

Fortunately, for those of you seeking the treasures of calm who don't want to go to the ends of the earth, and who aren't comfortable with immersing yourself in ancient rituals and spiritual traditions based in the language of foreign cultures, relief is at hand. Advances in human physiology, physics, psychology and education have given us practical confirmation that this special state exists, and that we can generate it whenever we choose. We can discover, develop and enjoy the skills for attaining **TRUE CALM** in our own language and at our own convenience.

***

WE ARE EVOLVING!

We can begin by discovering and using the natural control levers for our mind, body, emotions, and energy flow. As this author has learned, and as yogis throughout the centuries have known, all that is required to develop this control is to **carefully focus our attention.** **Attention-focusing** is our key to low-cost, low-maintenance, user-friendly, anytime-anywhere mastery of our arousal and calming systems.

The amazing degree of control we can accomplish by focusing our attention properly has been scientifically demonstrated in volumes of biofeedback research. A classic biofeedback experiment by Dr. John Basmajian proved that research subjects could directly learn to activate a single motor unit (that is, the individual neurons and the muscle fibers they supply with nerves) at will.[10] By listening to sounds that changed when the motor unit was turned on and when it was turned off, the subject gained such control that within minutes he could turn that motor unit on and off whenever he chose. The sounds acted as an auditory feedback for the body (bio), allowing subjects to focus their attention very precisely - enough to actually <u>feel</u> how to control that motor unit.

The field of biofeedback research represents a medical breakthrough of profound importance, the potential of which has not yet been fully explored. There's a huge possibility that almost nothing exists which we cannot control in our bodies through directing our attention-focusing. We won't always have biofeedback equipment handy, but we can gain immense control over our own body, mind and emotions without it. The quest is to locate and control the powerful physiological **focusing levers** which produce the desired results.

A better existence is beckoning us. Somewhere inside, **you already know it**. We need to bring it into existence **NOW**. So let's get started!

SURVIVING TO THRIVING

Surviving is from where we came
Human *THRIVING's* now the game
More joyous but unknown and strange
Our vehicle to here is change.

Fig. 1.9

CHAPTER TWO

LEARNING KEYS FOR TRUE CALM

"Enjoy yourself and try to learn. You will annoy someone.
And if you do not, you will annoy someone." Proverb[1]

*T*o accelerate your ability to gain the benefits of the state of **TRUE CALM**, and to insure that you complete this book achieving the lifelong skill of feeling calm - *within six seconds* - anytime and anyplace you want, I want to introduce certain tools that will help you learn these skills more easily.

Finding a single key, just like Nasrudin was looking for, will give you enormous control over the four body systems that produce all *Four Treasured Qualities*. This is the prized ability to...

FOCUS YOUR ATTENTION.

What does it mean to focus your attention? We think of attention-focusing as concentrating, thinking about something we want to think about. It also involves excluding things we don't want to focus on. More practically, we are referring to choosing which of our five senses we want to focus with and stay focused in. Generally, the more creative, happy, healthy and successful folks amongst us have cultivated this ability.

Focusing our attention is very sensual. It means using our senses to perceive. We sense. We see, we hear. We feel, we

ATTENTION-FOCUSING MODEL

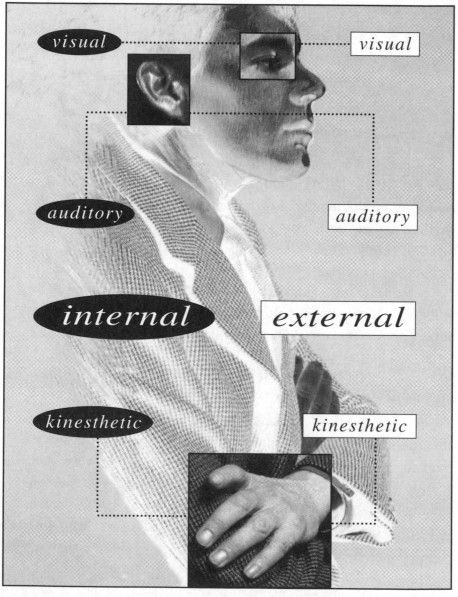

The three primary sensory modes: seeing, hearing and feeling, through which we perceive reality externally and internally during our daily activities.

Fig. 2.1

smell, we taste. Then we make sense of what we're sensing. This is how things make sense to us. Our aliveness increases when we add a new dimension to our sensual nature - being aware of what we are sensing AS we are sensing - because...

WE ARE SENSUAL, SENTIENT BEINGS.

We perceive reality through our five main senses. Yet, throughout our daily affairs, we mainly use only three of these: our senses of seeing, hearing and feeling. Using our eyes, ears and sense of touch, we can sense either externally (outside our body) or internally (inside our body). Throughout this book, the specific sense you want to focus with to more easily learn each **TRUE CALM** skill will be called the *"Preferred Focusing Sense."* Figure 2.1 shows how it will look. With this in mind, here's...

***

HOW TO SENSUALIZE YOURSELF

Seeing - External

After you've read these words, focus your eyes away from the page and look at your hands. See the various shades of colors of your skin, from your knuckles to your palms and fingernails. Notice the different textures of your skin, the creases, folds, rougher and smoother areas.

PREFERRED FOCUSING SENSE

external

Now look at your surroundings and notice all the colors around you, the objects, shapes, designs and sizes of everything you see. This is focusing your attention **externally** in the **visual** sensory mode.

Seeing - Internal

Picture inside your mind a beautiful purple rose, with a long emerald green and white candy-cane stem, with four turquoise leaves that have three sparkling gold stars apiece. Hold that image and try to see it more and more clearly.

Now let that image dissolve and make a picture of your own face with a mischievous grin on it. See yourself clearly. This is focusing your attention **internally** in the **visual** sensory mode.

Hearing - External

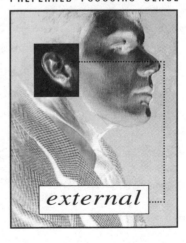

Focus on hearing all the sounds going on around you, wherever you are - at home, at work, indoors, outdoors, at the beach, in your car - wherever. Listen for everything you can hear: traffic, wind blowing through trees, motors humming, people talking, people walking, music, your own breathing - everything you are hearing. This is focusing your attention **externally** in the **auditory** sensory mode.

Hearing - Internal

Without making any sounds, say to yourself your name, phone number, home address. Now sing to yourself the first verse of your very favorite song. This is focusing your attention **internally** in the **auditory** sensory mode.

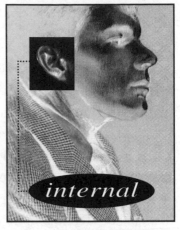

PREFERRED FOCUSING SENSE

internal

Feeling - External

Hold this book in your hands and notice the texture of its cover. Feel the thickness of the pages, and sense any differences between the temperature of your palms and the back of your hands. Feel the weight of your feet against the floor, or wherever they are resting. In doing this, you are focusing your attention **externally** in the **kinesthetic** sense - your sense of <u>touch</u>.

PREFERRED FOCUSING SENSE

external

Feeling - Internal

PREFERRED FOCUSING SENSE

internal

Take a deep breath and feel the air expanding your chest as the air fills your lungs. Now exhale and feel the air as it leaves your lungs, exiting your mouth or nose while you feel your chest contract back to normal. This is focusing your attention **internally** in the **kinesthetic** sensory mode - your sense of internal feeling. This is not "feeling" in terms of emotions, but in terms of touch, our tactile sense.

Notice how each of these sensory modes has a <u>slightly different</u> awareness to it, an unique consciousness. The state of mind, body, emotions and spirit we call "stress" is produced and maintained by doing certain specific things with our attention-focusing in each of these sensory modes. Producing the state of **TRUE CALM** - and feeling calm within six seconds - is simply a matter of focusing our attention in different ways within these three main senses.

It's easy!

Did you notice that when you were making the internal picture of the purple rose in your mind, you probably closed your eyes, looked up, looked away or let your eyes defocus to better see that image? At that moment you probably weren't able to clearly see your external environment at the same time. Also, when you were singing to yourself, you probably weren't hearing the sounds going on around you in your external environment. This give us a major key for gaining control over our attention-focusing, which is knowing that...

In any one sense, we cannot perceive both externally AND internally at the same time with clarity of focus.

We can go rapidly back and forth from internal to external in a single sense, but not both simultaneously with focus. Knowing some of the built-in qualities of attention-focusing gives us greater skill. We can gain **TRUE CALM** - and much more - simply by learning **how** to focus, **where** to focus, and, most importantly, **when** to focus.

If you were asked: "Why do you have eyes and ears?" you might answer: "to see and hear - to perceive." Yet the opposite is also true. Our sense organs also seem to have been designed to limit and restrict our perception, preventing us from perceiving more than a quite narrow range of sensory events.

For example, we see only the small visible portion of the entire light spectrum, what we call "visible light." We do not see x-rays, gamma rays, infrared and ultraviolet light without machines. We hear only a certain frequency range, not the higher vibrations of sounds that dogs and bats can hear.

Why are we so narrowly focused? We needed to achieve a major purpose: physical survival. This has required our focus to be stabilized with sensing physical events on our material plane: all the things we see, hear, feel, smell and taste. Seeing tigers and bears, hearing waterfalls and tasting which plants are good for us to eat enabled us to survive. If we were able to see all the other frequencies of light, we might be so mesmerized that hungry lions could just walk over and start munching on us.

Having accomplished physical realm survival on our planet Earth - knowing how to produce food, shelter and designer clothing - is a magnificent achievement. We did it! We are now free to advance, to expand our sensual nature by gaining mastery in the mental realm. The essence of operating mentally is attention-focusing.

Healthy attention-focusing involves the ability to move past the effects of physical survival responses.

We **can** focus our attention in precise ways that give us healthy control over the activities of our body, our mind, our emotions and our energy. In fact, our continued survival seems to require the ability to turn off our ancient fight/flight survival mechanism at will and to **turn on** our ancient calming mechanism. Just as clean water, air and food are needed for optimal physical realm health, *The Four Treasured Qualities - Presence of Mind, Emotional Peace, Physical Relaxation and Uplifting Energy* - are now crucial for optimal mental realm health.

Of course, *THRIVING* is what we want, beyond mere surviving. Once we can activate the state of **TRUE CALM**, many valuable new abilities can blossom. It's time!

To help with your focusing, each chapter will have a

KEY GOAL

For your growing pleasure, you will also encounter along the way a running metaphor of change as our vehicle for growth: the *Change Mobile*, with its zany drawings and poetry to better illustrate important concepts. So... are you ready?

KEY GOAL

LET'S GET CALM!

Fig. 2.2

CHAPTER THREE

EMOTIONAL PEACE

Treasured Quality #1

"Satisfaction is a treasure which does not decay." Proverb[1]

*T*he quiet pleasure of feeling calm is a delicious treat that stabilizes and rejuvenates our emotional life. Yet as wonderful as calm feels, and as nutritious as emotional peace is for our health and self-esteem, few people know how to feel calm at will. The first step in learning to achieve true calm is mastering...

THE DEEP "SIGH" BREATH

Try this:

- Find your pulse using the index and middle fingers on one hand. You can easily feel your pulse on the inside of your wrist, or on the side of your throat.

- Using the second hand of a clock or watch, count your heartbeats for a full 10 seconds. Write that number down, or remember it. (This number, multiplied by 6, is your rate of heartbeats per minute.)

- Sit up straight, but comfortably, in a chair that supports your back. Read the 4-step instructions that follow all the way through before you begin the exercise. Then, begin the Deep "Sigh" Breath.

Step 1. **DEEP INHALE.** Inhale deeply and smoothly, preferably through your nose, expanding your chest upwards and <u>outwards</u>, filling your whole torso and abdomen as you fill your lungs with air.

Step 2. **PASSIVE RELEASE.** Exhale by <u>letting go</u>, so the air comes out naturally.

You're neither forcibly pushing the air out, nor holding on by trying to exhale slowly. Exhale immediately after fully inhaling, so you're not holding your breath. Just... let go. Feel yourself getting out of the way. Let the air come out easily, at its own rate. Think of letting go of a balloon filled with air and watching the balloon flutter around the room as the air escapes at its own, natural speed.

Step 3. **REST.** After exhaling, rest as long as you **comfortably** can - until your body tells you that it's time to inhale again.

Focus your attention internally, feeling when your body signals you to breathe in again. Remember, you're listening to your body. Keep the muscles in your jaw, shoulders, arms and legs slack, or "let-go," like a limp dish rag, while you're in this rest period. Rest as long as you comfortably can. See how much you can let go. This rest period is "the pause that refreshes!"

Step 4. **REPEAT** THIS DEEP "SIGH" BREATH <u>6</u> TIMES, RESTING AFTER EXHALING. Inhale deeply. Try to let go a little more with your muscles each time you exhale, and stay relaxed a little longer after each exhalation. (See Figure 3.1)

Feel how long you can <u>comfortably</u> rest, until your body gives you the signal to inhale again. And, naturally...

ENJOY THE REST!

CONTINUE BREATHING SLOWLY AS YOU FIND YOUR PULSE. Count it again for 10 seconds. Compare this second number with the first one. Did your pulse rate go down? Great!

Every single decrease in the count represents a decrease in your heart activity of 6 heartbeats per minute. Even on their first attempt at the Deep "Sigh" Breath, most people find their heart rate decreases a few counts, or several! If your heart rate slowed between 2-5 counts, it means your pulse rate dropped 12-30 beats per minute. And you can improve that with practice! As you learn to focus your attention internally, in the feeling sense, you'll become expert in letting go.

You may notice your pulse seems quieter, or even harder to locate, after a period of Deep "Sigh" Breathing. **This means you also lowered your blood pressure.** Decreases in blood pressure frequently coincide with decreases in heartbeat. By letting go after exhaling, the smooth muscles of the blood vessel walls relax and open, allowing greater circulation with less pumping effort needed from the heart muscle.

On the other hand, you may feel and hear your heartbeat more strongly from inside your chest cavity. This is because when other noises in your body become quiet, your heart's constant movement becomes more perceptible.

DEEP "SIGH" BREATH

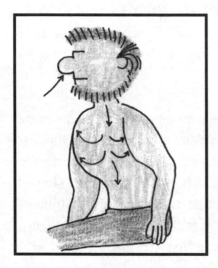

*Step 1. **Deep Inhale** - through the nose, as your chest expands upward and outward.*

*Step 2. **Passive Release** - exhale also through the nose by letting go.*

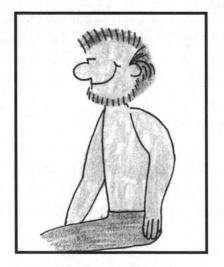

*Step 3. **Rest** - after exhale as long as is comfortable. Let-go.*

Fig. 3.1

Numbers and noises aside, how do you feel after Deep "Sigh" Breathing? Do you feel...

More relaxed?
And more calm?

Ask yourself, "How do I know I feel more relaxed and calm? What has changed?" **Have your muscles released?** Identify which muscles are now more relaxed. Those are muscles you were using more than was necessary as you sat and read this book. Those tense muscles use up valuable energy, constricting your circulation and leaving you feeling uncomfortable. The "letting go" allows our upper torso muscles to relax, so we need less blood and oxygen to fuel them. This also allows our heart and lungs to slow down. We reclaim our energy.

Did you feel a quieting of your mind? Most people also experience a release from mental "noise," as if a fresh ocean breeze has swept their thoughts out to sea. Rather than feeling confused, they report a new alertness and clarity of mind that's calming all by itself. Some people feel recharged from this. Do you?

Did you feel a sinking, slowing down sensation inside? You may have felt as if you were going toward sleep.

CULTIVATE THIS FEELING!

As we let go, this breathing pattern literally pushes us in the direction of sleep. That sinking, slowing-down sensation means you are literally shutting off your body's arousal system - like lifting your foot off the accelerator pedal of your car. This feeling tells you that you are turning on your body's calming system.

With the Deep "Sigh" Breath, you are taking advantage of a very natural bodily event. As soon as a big emotional experience is over, what's the first thing we do? We sigh. We've come to call this the "sigh of relief." Physiologically, it is actually a "sigh for relief."

The Deep "Sigh" Breath is designed to make your body transition mechanically from a state of high arousal (emotional upset) to a state of low arousal (emotional calm). When an emotional crisis passes, your body, in its wisdom, knows what to do. You no longer need to have all your systems in overdrive - that would be an inefficient use of energy. And so... you sigh! Correctly done, the Deep "Sigh" Breath imitates the benevolent function of a natural sigh. It gives you the conscious control you need to make your body relax and slow down, whenever you wish.

When people first learn this skill, they often exclaim: "But I always sigh when I'm stressed!" However, experience shows they usually didn't gain the refreshing benefits of the Deep "Sigh" Breath because they didn't <u>rest</u> - Step 3 - **after** exhaling. Instead of <u>feeling calm,</u> they inhaled immediately, and returned to a form of chest-breathing and breath-holding.

The two key steps in making the Deep "Sigh" Breath maneuver successful are:

1. **Fully "letting go"** during the exhale, and...
2. Lengthening the rest period by **continuing to "let go."**

When we remember these two elements, we can generate calmness quickly and easily every time. The Deep "Sigh" Breath must work because it is mechanical. Mimicking the postures, rhythms and movements you have associated over a lifetime with deep relaxation, calmness and sleep, it sends strong messages to your brain which say:

"Let's get calm"... and... "I am calm."

***

For a clearer understanding of this first step in the art of **TRUE CALM,** let's review some of the basic ways stress affects our breathing. Did you know there is a single pattern of breathing that maintains and even <u>produces</u> stress? It's called:

BREATH-HOLDING

The Breathing Pattern of Stress

If you were suddenly startled from behind by, say, a saber-toothed tiger, what is the very first reaction you would have? As you jump or turn around you would most likely inhale a quick gulp of air - <u>and hold it</u>. Walter Cannon, the great American physiologist who first identified the fight/flight emergency response, described this startle reaction of breath-holding as serving a great purpose. It quickly gives us some air, so if we need to fight or flee for our lives, we won't need to worry about breathing for a few crucial seconds![2]

Breath-holding can be wonderfully useful for survival purposes. It's also helpful for swimming underwater, for getting through smoke-filled rooms, and for those times when we're trapped behind a diesel-engine vehicle - or downwind from people with digestive problems. But breath-holding can <u>mechanically</u> trigger a chain of events in the body that regularly generates stress, the fight/flight responses, and even the most dreaded of stress reactions:

THE ANXIETY OR PANIC ATTACK!

Understanding how our breathing operates can give us much greater confidence under pressure, and can help us prevent much of our stress.

Because our fight/flight survival response evolved with us into the mental and emotional realms, simply focusing attention on our problems, doubts, fears and frustrations can automatically trigger breath-holding. (See Figure 3.2) That type of focus can easily provoke:

THE BREATHING PATTERN OF BREATH-HOLDING

1. Inhaling and holding the breath, using the chest to breathe
2. Exhaling
3. <u>Immediately</u> inhaling again, and <u>holding the breath</u>

If you are one of the many people who, when tense or anxious, experience tightness across your chest, dizziness, light-headedness, or scattered thinking, you are most likely holding your breath. You'll find it interesting to know what breath-holding can do to you mechanically.

When we hold our breath, we use a huge amount of muscle power to lift the heavy rib cage and shoulder bones, and hold them up. This inefficient effort involves muscles of the rib cage, pectorals, chest, shoulders, back muscles and even the muscles of the neck, throat and face. In order to perform the demanding job of keeping our chest held up and out, the muscles often tense and lock. One result is the feeling of tightness across the chest so commonly experienced during stress.

After these muscles become locked with tension, it becomes difficult to fully exhale, so we often begin taking rapid shallow breaths with our chests.

BREATH HOLDING

*Inhaling and holding the breath -
chest expands upward and outward*

Exhaling - often using the mouth

*Quickly inhaling again and hold-
ing the breath.*

Fig. 3.2

We call this "not being able to catch our breath." Because this posture of breath-holding imitates the breathing pattern we have used for millennia in actual life or death survival situations, it can, by itself, trigger emotional associations of anxiety and panic. The process then escalates.

Muscles are fueled by blood and oxygen, and our upper torso muscles act like gas guzzlers in a stress reaction. With lung expansion restricted in its downward motion, these muscles are not getting enough air. As they begin demanding more and more oxygen for fuel, our heart and lungs need to pump harder. In extreme cases, we start huffing and puffing, as we do when we've been exercising vigorously. Our chest starts heaving, signaling the end of our endurance. The brain, sensing an oxygen shortage is on the way, can then cause us to faint, simply to keep us from using up all the oxygen just for breathing.

Breath-holding even changes the chemistry of our blood.[3] Carbon dioxide is a natural waste product of muscle use, and we normally eliminate it from our blood by exhaling. But during fight/flight type stress, when we use so many upper torso muscles for breathing, we mass produce carbon dioxide. And because we are not properly exhaling and inhaling, carbon dioxide builds up, forming carbonic acid, which in turn makes our blood's pH more acidic.[4] Sensitive chemical sensors report this pH imbalance to the brain, which responds by slightly closing up the blood vessels which feed the brain itself.[5] While this constriction protects our brain's delicate fluid from the extra carbonic acid buildup, it also affects the brain's supply of blood and oxygen. Dizziness, light-headedness, mental confusion and scattered thinking can be the results.[6]

Finally, our brain wisely decides to make us start exhaling to eliminate the extra carbon dioxide in the blood. We hyperventilate, for the purpose of rebalancing our blood pH.[7] Sometimes the hyperventilation overshoots its goal, eliminating too much carbon dioxide, and we feel tingling sensations in our hands, feet and face. Numbness and muscle spasms can occur, with dizziness, or even loss of consciousness through fainting.[8] However, after a person faints, breathing and heart rates quickly return to normal. The mission is accomplished from the brain's point of view, much to the chagrin of the person who fainted.

The moral of this story is:

DON'T HOLD YOUR BREATH!!

Breath-holding is what NOT to do. (See Figure 3.3) Just by being aware of our breathing, especially during stress or emotional upset, we can prevent that whole chain reaction.

EXHALE PORTION OF BREATH CYCLE

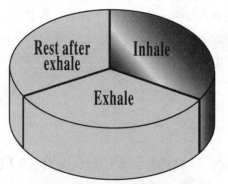

CALM BREATHING
(Deep "Sigh" Breath and Small Stomach "Sigh" Breath)

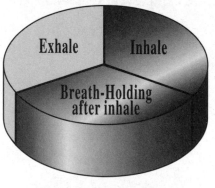

STRESS BREATHING
(Breath-Holding)

The main difference between breathing patterns which elicit calm and those which elicit stress is the relative portion of the breath cycle spent in exhalation. Calm breathing utilizes approximately 2/3 of each breath cycle for exhalation, versus only 1/3 for stress breathing.

Fig. 3.3

Examine the chart below and check off any of the symptoms you have experienced - once, or more than once. These are...

YOUR CHANGE AWARENESS SIGNALS

Breathing System

Changes in the activity of your internal organs:

Adrenaline rush

Heart racing

Pounding pulse

Perspiration

Rapid, shallow breath

Cold hands or feet

Face flushing

Stomach upset

Intense headache

Appetite gain or loss

Dry mouth

Stomach butterflies

Dizzy

Light-headed

Fig. 3.4

How many did you mark? One? Two? More? All of them? You're not alone! Those signals of stress are all delivered to you by...

YOUR AUTONOMIC NERVOUS SYSTEM

Our internal organs, such as our heart, lungs, glands and the hormones they produce, are all part of what we call our autonomic nervous system. This system operates nearly all of the automatic and supposedly involuntary behaviors of our bodies: heartbeat, circulation, respiration, blood pressure, metabolism, adrenaline, digestion, elimination, and so on. The autonomic nervous system consists of two main parts:

1. An <u>arousal</u> system - the sympathetic nervous system, and...
2. A **calming** system - the parasympathetic nervous system

The autonomic nervous system (ANS) has traditionally been called our "involuntary" nervous system because it generally runs automatically, outside of our conscious control. It was assumed to be uncontrollable by our conscious mind - by our willpower - simply because **people didn't know how to focus their attention in the proper "internal" ways to gain control**. When we focus our attention internally, which can be accomplished by practicing the skills in this book, **we can gain precise control over what was previously considered "involuntary" body activity**.

To feel calm, we simply switch off the arousal system, which generates stress, and we **turn on the calming system!** We accomplish that by focusing our attention internally, and using the appropriate levers for...

DOWNSHIFTING INTO CALM

The Deep "Sigh" Breath is the first tool in mastering **TRUE CALM**, mechanically reversing the process of breath-holding to produce a state of emotional peace. Once we've turned on our calming system, we can use a second breathing maneuver **to keep it on!** We call this:

***

The Small Stomach "Sigh" Breath

After doing several Deep "Sigh" Breaths, we no longer need to breathe deeply. We have just imbibed lots of oxygen. And with our muscles more relaxed, we need less oxygen anyway, and we don't need to exhale lots of carbon dioxide. We can begin taking smaller breaths - normal, quiet breaths. But instead of using our chest and upper torso to breathe, we now use our <u>stomach</u> area.

Remember, when air enters our lungs during the Deep "Sigh" Breath, our lungs expand upward and out. With this second breathing maneuver we simply allow our chest to remain "let-go," as it will be after the last Deep "Sigh" Breath, and we let the air enter our lungs, which now expand **downward** and outward. Our stomach pushes out as we inhale. This is called "diaphragmatic" breathing, or "quiet" breathing.

We begin with the same style and pattern of breathing you learned in the Deep "Sigh" Breath:

THE SMALL STOMACH "SIGH" BREATH

PREFERRED FOCUSING SENSE

internal

TAKE IN ONE DEEP "SIGH" BREATH to then let go with the chest, resting after exhaling as we learned earlier in this chapter. Then start the next stage of breathing....

Step 1. **NORMAL INHALE.** Inhale easily and smoothly, also through your nose, keeping your chest "let-go" and letting your <u>stomach</u> area fill up with air and expand out. This is not a large volume of air like the Deep "Sigh," but a smaller amount that feels comfortable.

Step 2. **PASSIVE RELEASE.** Release your breath like a "sigh," letting the air come out at its own natural rate.

Step 3. **REST**. After exhaling, rest as long as you **comfortably** can - until your body tells you it's time to inhale again. Focus your attention internally, **feeling** when your body gives you your signal to breathe in. Listen to your body. Keep your jaw, shoulders, arms and legs let-go while you're in this rest period. Continue to rest as long as you <u>comfortably</u> can. Feel how <u>much</u> you can let go. Enjoy your rest... and **enjoy the comfort your body brings you by letting go.**

Step 4. **REPEAT THIS FOR 20 BREATHS**. Allow your body to establish its own slow, steady breathing rhythm, by letting go and waiting for your signal to inhale again.

This breathing will soon become effortless. (See Figure 3.5) Instead of doing the breathing yourself, it's as if...

You are being breathed....

If distracting thoughts come into your mind, simply refocus your attention on...

- **feeling** your stomach moving...
- **feeling** the air enter and leave your lungs, and...
- **feeling** for your body's signal to inhale again.

Stay in the internal feeling sense as best you can.

This quiet, stomach breathing imitates the breathing patterns of babies, and of people in sleep - two <u>very</u> relaxed groups. When we choose to breathe like this, we send strong messages to our brain that say:

"Everything is fine...

You can relax...

Calm down...

Feel peaceful..."

***

THE BREATHING KEY

Breathing as the central focus of health has a long, fascinating history dating back thousands of years. In India, an ancient Hindu tradition contained thirty-two volumes written about "The Science of Breath." This body of knowledge was concerned with gaining precise control over both our human physiology and our mental states by using various breathing techniques. While much of this written learning was destroyed during religious wars centuries ago, it is being revived in books and by individuals who have tremendous working knowledge of this ancient teaching. For example, "pranayama" is a well-known technique in wide practice today.

Over four thousand years of study and experience, the Chinese have evolved a view of breath called **"chi,"** or life energy. **Chi** refers to more than simply oxygen, for the term also encompasses electromagnetic forms of energy found in the air. In the Chinese tradition, complex breathing maneuvers have been developed to increase this life energy, to circulate it directly to our internal organs, to strengthen and to vitalize specific body systems. This body of knowledge - often called **"chi gong,"** which means "producing life energy" - has traditionally been secret, guarded within certain families and passed on throughout generations. It is now being openly taught for health purposes in China and in the U.S.A. In fact, many Chinese medical doctors routinely use this healing force to treat illness.

SMALL STOMACH "SIGH" BREATH

Step 1. **Normal Inhale** - *through the nose. Stomach area expands outward. Chest stays "let-go."*

Step 2. **Passive Release** - *exhale also through the nose by letting go.*

Step 3. **Rest** - *after exhale as long as is comfortable. Let-go.*

Fig. 3.5

Hints of breathing being regarded as more than simply gas exchange in the lungs are found throughout the English language itself. Several clues point to a prior reverence for breathing, if not actual knowledge of its other uses. The words "spirit" and "spiritual" come from the Greek word "spiritos," which means breath. To be inspired, to inspire and receive inspiration, to "breathe life into" are experiences whose value is linked linguistically to the process of breathing.

At a more strictly physical level, our two most effective health-producing activities are aerobic exercise and relaxation. Their benefits have been well researched, and both hold in common a single, primary ingredient: <u>maintaining one's breathing at a steady rhythm for 20 minutes or more</u>. Let's compare the two.

Steady Breathing Rhythm - Fast Rate With Movement

Aerobic exercise, such as jogging, is designed to increase our heart rate for a prolonged period. When we reach this "training heart rate," which is about 80% of our maximal heart rate, and maintain it for 20 minutes or more, predictable health benefits occur.[9] Aerobic exercise helps lower fat (triglycerides) in the blood, strengthens the heart muscle itself, and increases our circulation, thus cleansing our system. It produces endorphins (natural pain killers and pleasure enhancers), and increases muscle fiber strength and neural efficiency. Aerobic exercise also shoots fresh oxygen into billions of cells in our body. The net effect is a kind of euphoria, the "runner's high." We feel great.

These benefits are usually examined with the heart muscle as the central focus. However, if we look at aerobic exercise with a focus on breathing, we can say that the movements of the various workouts serve to <u>increase our breathing rate and keep it increased at a steady rhythm</u>. Steady breathing over time allows the body to cleanse itself, to infuse billions of red blood cells with fresh oxygen, and to circulate this most important nutrient through the body, while eliminating metabolic waste products like carbon dioxide.

Clearly, the heart and lungs work together in this process. But the health benefits of this type of exercise fully blossom when the lungs have reached that faster but <u>steady rhythm</u> of breathing. This steady breathing rhythm also has a calming effect on mental activity, and is a major contributor to "the runner's high" - undoubtedly one of the joyful side effects of running.

Steady Breathing Rhythm - Slow Rate With No Movement

Breathing in a steady rhythm, <u>but at a slow rate</u>, generates a different set of extremely beneficial effects. Much research has already documented that slow, steady breathing activities such as meditation and deep relaxation produce an interesting array of health-giving changes in the human body - all of which demonstrate a <u>conserving</u> of energy.[10] Slow breathing seems to invoke the same rejuvenating and healing process that occurs when we rest an injured limb, recuperate after an illness, "cool down" after a strenuous workout, or just regroup after a rough day at the office.

These bodily changes include a slowing of internal organ activity by lowering oxygen consumption, carbon dioxide production, and the metabolic rate.[11] This alone provides a huge remedy to the destructive diseases of overactive, stressed organ systems which accelerate aging and weaken immune strength. Slow, steady breathing allows muscles to stay relaxed, thus reducing blood lactate, a product of muscle metabolism associated with anxiety.[12] Production of cholesterol, a controversial culprit in heart disease, is also lowered with this slow, steady breathing rate, while the autonomic nervous system slows down its arousal functions.[13]

These are precisely the healthy bodily changes that many of today's medications are designed to imitate. Slow, steady breathing provides benefits without dangerous side effects, dependency-producing qualities, or the high cost of pharmacological intervention. The number of people dependent upon pills, drugs and alcohol to fall asleep, reduce anxiety, lower blood pressure, relieve headaches, or simply relax is staggering. Those numbers clearly point to the need for learning to use our calming skills to produce greater states of health in a natural way.

Quiet breathing is probably the most efficient type of breathing we can do - unless we're really exerting ourselves strenuously - for several reasons.[14] When correctly done, it uses but a single muscle, the diaphragm muscle, which stretches across the bottom of the rib cage and pulls down as we inhale. All the other chest, torso and shoulder muscles get to rest.

Stomach or diaphragmatic breathing also makes optimal use of gravity. When we are sitting or standing, which we do for most of our waking hours - and especially when we're stressed - the blood flowing through our lungs is drawn by gravity toward the bottom third of our lungs.[15] If we breathe shallowly, predominantly using our upper chest for oxygen exchange, while our blood is flowing mainly in the bottom part of our lungs, we have a poor mixing of air and blood. Our heart and lungs have to work overtime, pumping harder to deliver oxygenated blood to our body. However, when we do the Small Stomach "Sigh" Breath, we are mechanically sending air <u>directly</u> to the lower part of our lungs where the blood flows, producing a more thorough mix of air and blood. Our heart and lungs get to slow down and work less. We get more oxygen with less effort! (See Figure 3.6)

Breathing at a slow, steady rate also alters brain function beneficially, producing the slower "alpha" waves characterized by increases in amplitude (intensity) and regularity typical of a state of calm.[16] People in this alpha state regularly report greater creativity, new insights and relief from racing thoughts. Slow breathing seems to open gateways inside our minds, allowing easier access to intuitive thought. Many people report marked <u>increases</u> in intuition as their experience with the alpha state continues.[17]

Together these wonderful, physiological changes are signs of the mind/body/energy state known as...

EMOTIONAL PEACE

When we spend time in this relaxed, alert state, we feel a sense of quiet pleasure, joy and well-being that has no comparison. It is probable that slow, steady breathing increases the body's natural production of endorphins. With those pleasure-enhancing, pain-killing hormones flowing through our body, with our brain waves tuned to receive more creative, intuitive sense perceptions, with our muscles relaxed, and with our internal organs on low idle, we can fully enjoy this refreshing state that literally increases our health.

GRAVITY AND BLOOD FLOW IN THE LUNGS

When sitting or standing, blood flows mainly to the lower lobes of the lungs. Diaphragmatic, or stomach breathing, sends inhaled air directly to this area of greater blood flow, resulting in more efficient gas exhange and less work for the heart, lungs and muscles used for breathing. *(Adapted from Shapiro, 1973.)

Fig. 3.6

These health benefits will be receiving long-deserved attention as our civilization evolves, for we need these gifts to move beyond the patterns of mere surviving into accomplishing our greater potential for *THRIVING*.

***

HOW TO PRACTICE

Practicing the sequence of breathing for **TRUE CALM** takes only 3-4 minutes. You can extend the practice time just by doing more Small Stomach "Sigh" Breaths. Best results occur if you practice <u>a minimum of 4 separate times</u> during the day when you are first learning. More is even better. Your goal is to make this beneficial breathing skill an automatic part of your daily routine.

Remember to put the two breathing maneuvers together, and do both, in this sequence:

Step 1. **DO 3 - 6 DEEP "SIGH" BREATHS**. <u>Rest</u> each time after exhaling.

Step 2. **DO 20 OR MORE SMALL STOMACH "SIGH" BREATHS**. <u>Rest</u> each time after exhaling.

You will probably notice that your accustomed style of breathing is with your chest. With just a few days of practice, frequently "tuning in" to how you are breathing, then changing to stomach breathing as you need to, you will find you somehow begin to do this quiet breathing automatically. It will soon become your normal style of breathing, and your body will love you for trying! It seems we humans are designed to stomach breathe as a normal pattern for nearly every activity that isn't strenuous exercise or fight/flight behavior. Because this quiet stomach breathing is perhaps the most efficient breathing we can do, our bodies will help us learn it quickly. And you will find it most useful in helping you...

FEEL CALM IN STRESSFUL SITUATIONS....

Sometimes we are in public when our **awareness of change** powerfully grabs our attention, producing stress and anxiety in our bodies. We can't always stop and perform 26 breaths. One sigh is socially acceptable. Two or more deep sighs are suspicious! However...

You can always do a single "Deep Sigh Breath" to turn on your calming system, and follow it up with Small Stomach "Sighs" to maintain calm.

You'll be quietly taking control of yourself and making your body generate calm. Finally, your ability to feel calm whenever you wish, no matter what chaos is going on around you, depends on one thing:

KNOWING WHAT TO DO SO WELL
THAT YOU JUST DO IT!

Practice doing the 26 breaths four times daily for four weeks. These breathing skills mechanically give you the physical foundation for *Emotional Peace - Treasured Quality #1*. **Practice and you will gain a marvelous tool to achieve calm and emotional peace for a lifetime!** But you do have to remember to put in the initial effort.

***

You have now learned the first and most basic maneuver of **TRUE CALM.** There are three more to come. You're on your way to mastering the six-second skill of *instant calm.* Keep breathing... and keep reading!

KEY GOAL

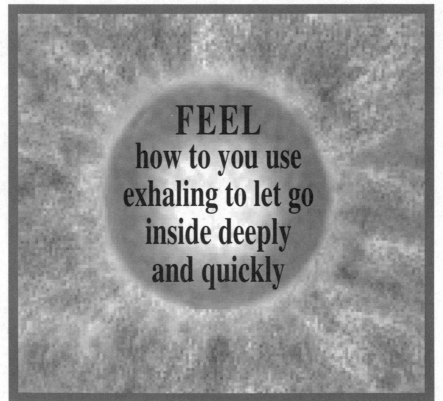

FEEL
how to you use
exhaling to let go
inside deeply
and quickly

Fig. 3.7

PHYSICAL RELAXATION

Treasured Quality #2

"If you cannot lie down, you will stand up once too often." Proverb[1]

When we think of using our muscles, what usually comes to mind are various forms of physical work - lifting and hauling - or activities like running, weightlifting, tennis and other sports. The quest for firm, well-defined muscles, the desire to appear and be strong, and the benefits of endurance usually grow from exercises involving repeated muscle contractions. Vigorously tensing and working our muscles through pulling, pushing and swinging have become synonymous with good health.

Yet there is an equally important and often overlooked use of muscles, one which becomes more and more valuable as we grow and mature. This different muscle use requires learning how to make our muscles loosen and relax. Muscles function two ways: they contract and they release. They tense and they let go. True muscle health includes activities of releasing as well as contracting. In fact...

MUSCLES ARE OUR MAIN TOOLS
FOR RELAXING!

Although nutrition, exercise and basic lifestyle are considered the biggest contributors to health problems, overly tight muscles resulting from stress are also frequent contributors to many maladies. One of the most common problems of overly contracted muscles is the tension headache. Experienced as a vice-like tightness in the temples, and extending around the sides of the head, the common tension headache has many people turning to various drugs for relief. Once you know the release levers for the temple muscles, however, that headache is most easily aborted and prevented altogether.

Try this:
- Place your fingertip on your temples.
- Clench your jaw and feel the muscles in the temple area contract.
- Now... release your jaw and feel those same muscles relax.

Perhaps the only way to tighten our temple muscles is to tighten our master or jaw muscles - by clenching the jaw, by grinding our teeth, or even by chewing gum. This means that virtually all tension headaches originating in the temple area can be quickly dissolved by releasing those muscles. Relief is often as easy as letting the jaw drop, and keeping it in a "let-go" position for 60 seconds - much faster, cheaper and safer than taking a muscle relaxer.

Even migraine headaches can many times be traced back to a pattern begun with tightening the jaw and other face muscles, which puts pressure on the sensitive blood vessels and the nerves around them. This pressure can produce painful contracting and expanding reactions in the blood vessel walls. Certain migraine headaches can be prevented by mechanically releasing those same facial muscles, especially if you catch them early, before the reaction pattern leading to migraine gets underway. That provides us with a clue to the link between...

FACE MUSCLES AND OUR
MENTAL ACTIVITY

Intimate connections exist between our facial muscles, our thoughts and our feelings. So intimate are those connections that every expression, each feeling and nearly every thought, especially if it carries an emotional zing, is immediately reflected in our facial muscles. The simple fact is...

We relate to the world primarily through our face.

Why? Because four of our five major sense organs are located on our face. Our eyes, ears, nose and mouth are all performing their jobs of perception on our face, feeding back enormous amounts of information to our brain, especially perceptions necessary for our survival. These connections instantly move our muscles into expressions that become automatic. Some emotions cause certain muscles to contract, while others allow those same or other muscles to release.

Concern and concentration tighten the forehead muscles into furrows. Surprise raises our eyebrows. Fear makes our eyes widen, while happy thoughts of joy and mischief let them sparkle. Humor stretches our mouth as our cheeks lift up. Frowns of discouragement push those same cheek muscles downward. Suspicion can raise a single eyebrow, while acceptance might lift the other. Astonishment and disbelief can make our jaw drop open. Determination and anger grip the jaw closed, clenching our teeth together as if ancient memories of using our jaw as a weapon reside in those muscles.

It's probable that these associations took at least a lifetime to produce, and that some, like clenching the jaw, are the result of eons of muscle memory. A lifetime of tense muscles resulting from stress, anxiety, emotional upset and anger has conditioned our facial muscles - especially the jaw, the forehead and the muscles surrounding the eyes - to readily contract. When they do contract, our brains receive a message which says: "Danger! Warning! Something's wrong out there!"

The muscle/mind postural association works both ways. If we consciously tense our face muscles for a few minutes, placing them in the posture of tension, we soon begin thinking stressful thoughts and having feelings of emotional discomfort. It's fairly mechanical. Knowing this, **we can also take advantage of these interconnections, and make them work for us!**

An easy and powerful way to change our mind/body state from one of distressed panic into calm is to release our facial muscles, especially the jaw. This sends a strong, clear message to our brain that says:

"Everything is fine. Relax."

Then the rest of us - our emotions, thoughts and physiology - all become more calm and more comfortable. Throughout our lifetime, whenever we were feeling calm, peaceful and safe, our face muscles were released and relaxed. We can invoke these healthy and desirable muscle associations mechanically, by releasing our facial muscles, and letting them remain let-go in the muscle postures of calm. It works! And the great news is...

THE SAME PRINCIPLE WORKS
FOR THE REST OF YOUR BODY!

Our confidence level, our mental activity, our emotional states, and even our sense of well-being are all influenced by the state of our muscles. When our skeletal muscles are relaxed, we have quicker reflexes. As any athlete will affirm, relaxed readiness is quicker and more energy efficient than tensed readiness.

Having our muscles loose can contribute to our feeling more open to change, more welcoming to new ideas, more confident in situations that once seemed threatening - like giving a speech to a group of people. A state of muscle relaxation lifts our spirit, giving us a desirable, casual attitude about even our most pressing concerns. When other people perceive us as calm and relaxed, particularly in pressure situations, they feel greater respect, increased trust and more confidence in us. At the executive level of corporate life, the ability to handle pressure is increasingly considered a key factor in recruitment and hiring decisions.

On the other hand, worrying and dwelling on our problems often makes muscles throughout our bodies become racked with tension - resulting in headaches, raised shoulders, neck pain, lower back pain, knots in our stomachs and clenched jaws. Being "uptight" can potentially ruin our negotiating power in business situations, for others spot nervous tension as a sign of weaker bargaining position. Tense muscles are a distraction to mental clarity, and can make us seem socially awkward, even inept. One clumsy mistake in a social setting can take us the entire evening to recover from, plaguing our thoughts for hours. And the costs of muscle tension can go far beyond social awkwardness.

Health Dangers of Tense Muscles

Though muscles can both contract and release, under stress muscles seem to react in only one way: they contract. Stress is a primary cause of prolonged muscle contraction. Stomach knots, cramps, lower back pain and chest tightness can often be the effects of stress on the skeletal muscles. Excessive teeth grinding and jaw clenching can not only wear down the teeth, but can wreak havoc on the mouth, eventually contributing to TMJ, or temperomandibular joint dysfunction. The number of decent folks who grind their teeth at night, needing tooth guards and dental work and often awakening with sore gums, is enormous and growing. Keeping our muscles unnecessarily tense, especially the larger skeletal muscle groups, is an enormous drain of energy, using up valuable nutrients which could be used for other purposes.

Over time tight muscles in the neck and shoulders can pinch nerves and push vertebrae out of proper alignment, leading to pressure on the disks, eventually accelerating the process of disk inflammation and degeneration. A multitude of problems can develop when proper nerve flow is impeded, since our nerves carry crucial information every organ in our body needs to operate in good health. Our joints can become stiff and immobile when muscles around them are constricted for too long, even blocking the flow of vital fluids and blood needed for flexibility. Some forms of arthritis develop more easily under these conditions of prolonged muscle contraction.

Incredible amounts of drugs, pills and alcoholic concoctions are consumed to satisfy our craving for muscle release, and many of these come with dangerous side effects, including depression, lowered confidence or addiction. One measure of how important *Physical Relaxation* has become is the increasing number of costly programs, fancy spa vacations and gimmicky merchandise being advertised to offer relief from muscle tension. This is a ridiculously urgent testimony for what's missing: the simple ability to physically relax our own muscles. (See Figure 4.1)

Knowing WHEN our muscles are becoming unnecessarily tight, WHICH muscles are tightening, and HOW to calm tense muscles is tremendously important for good health. Releasing our muscles rejuvenates us by restoring the energy being wasted on unproductive muscle contraction.

MUSCLES

Muscles are our grounding gear
They mobilize for anger/fear
Tension, headaches, jaws clenched tight
Stiff joints result when not used right
Releasing muscles frees all these
We then can feel TRUE CALM with ease.

Fig. 4.1

Releasing our muscles helps to heal us by opening the flow of blood and the nutrients it circulates. Relaxed muscles conserve our energy for when we really need it.

Review the chart below and check off the symptoms of muscle tension you have experienced, either infrequently or... most of the time.

YOUR CHANGE AWARENESS SIGNALS

Muscle **S**ystem

Tensed, cramped or tight muscles in these body areas:

Forehead	*Shoulders*
Temples	*Chest tightness*
Eyes	*Stomach knots*
Clenched jaw	*Lower back*
Teeth grinding	*Thighs*
Neck/throat	*Calves*
Arms/hands	*Feet, toes*

Fig. 4.2

Exhausting, isn't it? But help is on the way! Because...

Just as our muscles have a mechanism for tensing, they each have a mechanism for releasing!

Remember the kinesthetic external and internal focusing exercise you learned in the **Learning Keys to TRUE CALM**? The following exercise is similar. It involves your focus on **feeling.**

By focusing our attention internally in the kinesthetic or feeling sense, we can locate the levers for mechanically releasing the tension in our muscles and thus learn how to relax our skeletal muscles quickly and deeply. It's simply a matter of knowing where to focus, knowing what to do with that focus, and...

PREFERRED FOCUSING SENSE

internal

***

"LETTING GO"

Following are two exercises for finding and using the levers that release the <u>nine major muscles groups</u> involved in tension, headaches and stress reactions. Mastering these exercises - they're <u>easy</u> - gives you the ability to release these muscle levers <u>whenever you want</u>. Focus on recognizing when YOUR muscles are tense (contracted) and when they are relaxed (released). While some people may want to visualize the muscle releasing, like a knotted rope unwinding and loosening, your control is most direct when you concentrate on:

ACTIVE MUSCLE RELAXATION[2]

While you can certainly perform this exercise lying in bed before going to sleep, it is best to familiarize yourself with it when sitting upright in a chair with your heels resting on the floor. Be sure to keep all other muscles relaxed <u>except the one you're tensing</u>, so you learn to separate different muscles. Here's the key to lifelong control:

Keep your attention focused on feeling each muscle group relax for the full 10 seconds by <u>continuing to let go more and more</u>....

- **Tense each muscle group for 5 seconds.**
- **Release each muscle group for 10 seconds.**

PREFERRED FOCUSING SENSE

internal

Step 1. Feet and calves - **Tense** by pulling back on your ankles, bending them as if you're trying to touch your toes to your shins. **Release.** Focus on **feeling** your calf and feet muscles relaxing by **let**ting **go** more and more.

Step 2. ***Thighs*** - **Tense** by straightening and lifting your legs parallel to the floor, using only your thigh muscles while keeping your feet and calf muscles let-go. **Release.** Focus on **feeling** your thigh muscles relaxing more and more by **let**ting **go**.

Step 3. ***Buttocks*** - **Tense** by squeezing your buttocks together, lifting yourself off the chair somewhat. **Release** and let go. **Feel** your weight against the chair. Feel the chair support your body by **let**ting **go**.

Step 4. ***Stomach*** - **Tense** by tightening your stomach muscles, as if you're preventing something from pushing against your stomach. **Release**. **Feel** your stomach muscles relax by **let**ting **go** more and more.

For the rest of the exercise, use the Small Stomach "Sigh" Breaths to keep your stomach muscles relaxed.

Step 5. ***Arms and hands*** **- Tense** by making fists and flexing all the muscles in your forearms and upper arms at the same time. (Keep your jaw let-go!) **Release. Feel** those muscles in your hands and arms relax by **let**ting **go** more and more. Feel the weight of your arms and hands relax against whatever they are resting.

Step 6. ***Shoulders*** **- Tense** by pushing your shoulders straight up towards your ears, as high as they will go, not pushing them forward or backward, just upward. **Release** by dropping your shoulders. **Feel** them relax more and more by **let**ting **go**. Concentrate on feeling your shoulders resting by their own weight.

Step 7. ***Neck stretch*** **- Stretch** by pushing your shoulder blades together and at the same time pushing your chin up and out at a 45 degree angle. **Release.** Focus on **feeling** your shoulders resting comfortably by their own weight while **let**ting **go** with the jaw and returning your chin to its normal position.[3]

Step 8. ***Mouth and jaw*** **-** Keeping your teeth slightly apart, **tense** these muscles by forcing a big smile. **Release.** Focus on **feeling** your jaw drop, especially from the back of your jaw. Relax by letting your jaw just hang by its own weight, **let**ting **go** more and more. (This is a great thing to do to fall asleep quickly, or while walking, driving, reading and listening to others talk.)

*Step 9. **Eyes and cheeks** - **Tense** by squinching your eyes tightly shut. **Release**. Focus on **feeling** your cheek muscles and the muscles around your eyes relaxing by **let**ting them **go** more and more.

*Step 10. **Forehead** - **Tense** by pushing your eyebrows up as high as they will go. **Release**. Focus on **feeling** your forehead muscles relax more and more by **let**ting **go** with your eyebrows.

• **Without moving anything**, mentally go back down your body, **releasing a little more** each muscle group you just relaxed: forehead, eyes, jaw, shoulders, arms, hands, stomach, thighs, calves and feet. Do this simply by focusing on **let**ting **go**, by not tensing at all. Now **feel** what your body feels like by letting go and...

MEMORIZE THIS FEELING!

Concentrate on <u>remembering</u> how this feels, so each time you practice, and whenever you want to relax, you know exactly where your release levers are. All it takes is practice.

Enjoy the comfort your body brings you
by letting go....

***

Keep in mind that this state of *Physical Relaxation*, which you produce by letting go the muscle release levers, is a powerful healing state for your body and mind, as well as for your emotions. It is similar to what happens when a cast is put on a broken arm, allowing all the energy, blood and nutrients circulating through that area to be utilized fully for healing, not for movement.

This is a major reason why doctors so often prescribe rest. When the body is in this state of calm, its energy can go toward healing, toward recharging itself. It is as if our internal organs all come into homeostasis, into a healthy synchronization with each other, allowing our energy to be regenerated.

With practice we can relax even more deeply than sleep **while staying fully alert**. We can gain the recharging benefits of a two hour nap in just a few minutes. It's not a matter of how long we relax, but how deeply we release. Cultivating this *Physical Relaxation* also rejuvenates our emotions, our spirits, and our mental clarity.

***

HOW TO PRACTICE

The best way to quickly master your control over the muscle release levers is to practice this <u>once daily for at least one week</u>. It will prepare you to perform the second, faster muscle relaxation skill you are about to learn, which requires that you already know your release levers. That second exercise is a must for performing the six-second *instant calm* skill itself.

Sandwich this muscle relaxation exercise <u>in between the two breathing maneuvers once daily</u>, so that you do <u>6</u> Deep "Sigh" Breaths, then the active muscle relaxation, and then the <u>20</u> Small Stomach "Sigh" Breaths. **Your reward:**

FEEL THE COMFORT YOUR BODY BRINGS YOU AFTER HAVING LET GO WHILE YOU ARE ENJOYING THE STOMACH "SIGH" BREATHS.

There will probably be stressful times when you may feel tense or uptight. From having practiced this exercise, you can know exactly which of your muscles are tensed and you can release them directly. This saves time since in general only a few muscle groups contract during stress, not the whole body. Feel which ones are tensed, tense them more, and then release. You will then quickly be able to learn:

***

PASSIVE MUSCLE RELAXATION

After practicing the active muscle relaxation exercise for a week, you will find it easy to relax your muscles just by using the release levers - without needing to first tense the muscles. This second exercise is designed to make use of the release levers to accomplish <u>faster</u>, deeper muscle relaxation. This time we'll start with the forehead and relax our body, going from head to feet. Notice the powerful relaxation effect you can feel just by relaxing your facial muscles!

*Step 1. **Forehead** -* **Feel** which are your forehead muscles by slightly raising your eyebrows or wiggling them a bit. Now **release** your forehead muscles, relaxing by **letting go** with your eyebrows. Focus on **feeling** the weight of your eyebrows, letting them sink and rest comfortably by their own weight.

PREFERRED FOCUSING SENSE

internal

Step 2. **Eyelids** - **Release** your eyelids by letting your eyelids close. Relax more deeply by **feeling** the weight of your eyelids resting comfortably by their own weight as you **let go** more and more.

Step 3. **Eyeballs** - With your eyelids closed, find the position in which your eyes **feel** most comfortable, the least strained. This is generally somewhere in a center position, perhaps looking down a little. Then, **release** your eyes and just let them rest quietly in this position, without moving. Let them remain still for the rest of the exercise by **let**ting **go**. This is a most important calming key, because the more our eyes are moving - even when our lids are closed - the more we are thinking. Making the eyes still also helps clear our mind and is great for falling asleep.

Step 4. **Cheeks and jaw** - **Feel** the muscles you use to smile and talk. Now **release** your jaw and cheek muscles by letting your jaw drop, especially from the back of the jaw, while letting your lips slightly touch with your teeth apart. Focus on **feeling** the weight of your jaw, and letting it rest comfortably by its own weight. Feel your whole face relaxing in this **let-go** position. (Releasing these four facial muscle groups can give you a wonderfully rich feeling of relaxation, which is especially good for quieting the mind and entering sleep.)

Step 5. **Shoulders** - **Feel** which are your shoulder muscles and **release** them by **let**ting **go** with your shoulders, letting them drop and rest comfortably by their own weight. (Make an effort to routinely go through your day with your shoulders released and resting in this position. It prevents muscle tension from building up in this important area and can prevent the problems of neck pain and headaches due to prolonged muscle tightness in this area.)

Step 6. ***Arms and hands*** - **Feel** your arms and hands and **release** these muscles by letting go, allowing your arms and hands to rest comfortably by their own weight in your lap, or against the chair. Feel the weight of your limbs resting against whatever is supporting them. Continue to **let go** more and more.

Step 7. ***Thighs*** - **Feel** the weight of your thighs resting against the chair you're sitting in. **Release** your thigh muscles by **let**-ting them **go** more and more, allowing the chair to support them.

Step 8. ***Feet and calves*** - **Feel** the weight of your feet against the floor and **release** them by **let**ting **go**, letting the floor support their weight.

• **Mentally repeat this process**, focusing again at the forehead, then going down your body and relaxing by <u>letting go a little more with each release lever</u>. Keeping your muscles released, do the 20 Small Stomach "Sigh" Breaths, enjoying the rest each time after you exhale.

ENJOY THE COMFORT YOUR BODY BRINGS YOU BY LETTING GO.

***

After learning this passive relaxation exercise, you now have the choice of relaxing your muscles by either procedure. Sometimes, if we're really uptight and "wired," we can more effectively calm ourselves by putting these together.

• **First, do 6 Deep "Sigh" Breaths.**

- **Follow this with active muscle relaxation.**
- **Then do the passive relaxation exercise back <u>down</u> the body.**
- **Finally, do <u>20</u> or more Small Stomach "Sigh" Breaths to <u>stay deeply relaxed</u>.**

With practice, you'll find that relaxed muscles enable you to think better, focus more clearly, and make more astute decisions in your work. Relaxed muscles produce a greater happiness in your daily life. You'll sleep better - when you <u>choose</u> to sleep - and you'll find you have vastly more energy at the end of your day!

***

You now have learned the first <u>two</u> *Treasured Qualities* in the mastery of **TRUE CALM.** You're halfway home to mastering the six-second skill of *instant calm*. Hasn't it been easy so far? And your pleasure is about to increase <u>dramatically</u>. Keep breathing, and stay let-go.

THE BEST IS YET TO COME!

KEY GOAL

FEEL
how to
release each
muscle group

Fig. 4.3

CHAPTER FIVE

PRESENCE OF MIND
Treasured Quality #3

"It is the readiness of the mind that is wisdom."[1]

*T*he governor of a midwestern state once told me he was always thinking about many things at once, constantly planning and organizing the huge workload of managing his state. He confided that this remarkable efficiency had become such a driving force that one time he had skied down the most beautiful slopes in Vail, Colorado and afterward, when he heard everyone else marveling at the beauty of the mountains, he realized that he hadn't seen a thing. He couldn't recall a single detail! Wherever he was mentally based, it was <u>not</u> in the present.

When he learned the skill for **Presence of Mind**, it was like a religious experience for him! He enthusiastically shared with me that he had been outside in the yard, and for the first time in many years had actually heard birds chirping in the trees. Like an excited child at a circus, he described how he had heard the wind blowing through the leaves. Learning the skill for **Presence of Mind** released him from being at the mercy of whatever thoughts entered his mind and of his constant mental chatter. He learned how to feel more alive by becoming more aware, and he learned that living in the present is a gift he could award himself <u>at any time</u>. He learned that...

Presence of Mind is the timing key for being fully alive.

Presence of Mind involves perceiving through our senses of hearing, feeling, seeing, smelling and tasting with the added quality of **being aware** of what's being perceived AS it is being perceived. It is a passive receiving of sensory information that is experienced in the moment, while it is occurring - **NOW**. That includes what's going on around us, and what's going on inside of us. People with *Presence of Mind* are constantly "tuned in" to this ongoing stream of sensory events.[2]

The single most important tool for achieving *Presence of Mind* is:

***

ATTENTION-FOCUSING

Presence of Mind seems to be a scarce commodity in our time. Too many people too often seem to be more absent than present - as if they are "not all there." Especially when **there** is really **here**. As usual, the root cause seems to be stress, the greatest single enemy of *Presence of Mind*.

We have already briefly explored attention-focusing in Chapter Two, "**Learning Keys For TRUE CALM.**" For a fuller demonstration, let's focus our attention in ways that are <u>opposite</u> to how we focus during stress.

Visual-External or "Looking Outside":

- **Close your eyes** (after reading these instructions), and face in a different direction. Then open your eyes for <u>one second</u>, and immediately close them again.

PREFERRED FOCUSING SENSE

external

- **Name everything you saw** in as much detail as possible: colors, objects, shapes, textures, background, foreground.

- **Keeping your eyes closed, face another direction**. Open your eyes for one second and immediately close them. Now describe what you just saw in great detail. Repeat this <u>3</u> times total.

- **Notice how you feel** after doing this.

Couples can have fun with this. One person can lead the "viewer" by the arm until there's something interesting to see. After a one-second glance, the viewer can describe what was observed to the guide. Switch roles after three descriptions. Or you can do this exercise alone, even in a familiar spot in your home or office. You'll be amazed at what is revealed to you.

Kinesthetic-External or "Feeling Outside":

PREFERRED FOCUSING SENSE

external

- **With your eyes closed, begin focusing** on your feet, and **name** everything you are feeling with your feet - not internal sensations such as muscle twinges, but external sensations, like what you are feeling against your skin, and the pressure of each article of clothing on your body.

If you are seated, can you feel the weight of your feet against the floor? Are you feeling your shoes on your feet, and the tops of your shoes resting near your ankle? Can you feel the tops of your socks on your legs, or the weight of your pants or skirt against your calves, knees and thighs? And so on.

- **Slowly proceed up your body, focusing** on each body area. Name to yourself every sensation you are feeling with the skin of that body part AS you are feeling it. Stay focused in your external feeling or kinesthetic sense.

Include your whole body - your feet, calves, knees, thighs, stomach, back, chest, hands, arms, shoulders, neck, the back of your head and your face.

Couples can do this together by having one person close their eyes and name every sensation out loud to the partner who has his or her eyes open. If you see that your partner skipped something, like naming the watch on their wrist, ask them to focus again on feeling their wrist. If you hear your partner naming an internal bodily sensation, ask them to focus on what they are feeling externally - against their skin - on that area of their body. After exploring the whole body, switch roles.

Auditory-External or "Hearing Outside":

- **Keeping your eyes closed, focus** your full attention on all the information your ears are bringing you. **Name** each and every sound in your external environment, in the room with you, outside of the room, and even outside of the building you're in. Continue naming each sound, even if it repeats, so you are fully aware of all sounds around you. Report each sound fresh AS it occurs. **Do this continuously for 3 minutes.**

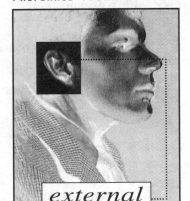

PREFERRED FOCUSING SENSE

external

Name each sound briefly, with no interpretations, no comments, judgments or long descriptions. If you don't recognize a particular sound, just say: "click, thump, noise, etc." Become an objective reporter, simply noting each and every sound as it presents itself. (Couples can take turns naming the sounds out loud to each other.)

How do you feel? Comparing how you feel <u>now</u> with how you felt <u>before</u> you began this exercise, what do you notice that's different?

If you didn't actually try this exercise (caught you!), please do yourself a favor: <u>Stop reading now!</u> <u>Go back and really do it!</u> Otherwise, you will be prejudiced by reading about it, and you will have cheated yourself of a pure and rich original experience that you'll want to have. Now - having completed this exercise... **how do you feel?**

- Are you **more aware** now of things going on around you? Less aware? Or the same?
- Are you feeling big emotions, little emotions, or **no emotions**?
- Are you thinking many thoughts, or **really not thinking at all?**

Answering these questions honestly will give you insight into the special qualities of *Presence of Mind*. If you fully concentrated on the exercises, you probably are much more aware of things going on around you. You probably feel no strong emotions or feel emotionally neutral for the moment. You probably are not "thinking" anything, but are "perceiving."

If you didn't experience these qualities, go back and do the last part, focusing your attention fully in the auditory external sense <u>for a full 3 minutes</u>. Just listen intently and name all sounds you hear around you AS they occur. And when you've finished, you can tell yourself...

WELCOME TO THE PRESENT!

Presence of Mind is an elusive mental vitamin that energizes us with greater sensory awareness and richer mental clarity. This is very important to cultivate, because life happens NOW - in the present. Life does not happen in the past or future. When something happened in the past, it actually happened in the present. Future events will also happen in the present. Everything happens in the present. It is only our minds which fool us into leaving the present, our home base in time. The present is our position of greatest personal power, for right now is when we decide to think about, take action, and choose what we want MORE OF in our life.

Thinking clearly while fully focusing our attention on whatever we want greatly improves our concentration and our learning capacities. *Presence of Mind* brings with it an ability to see more of "the big picture," to sense what's the correct thing to say, do or be in any given situation.

People with *Presence of Mind* seem to be more intuitive, more creative, and more open to change. These folks share the characteristic of being "centered," or more grounded. They are the ones we want to have around in emergencies, for they are the coolheaded among us, gifted with a sharper awareness. They seem unflustered by whatever turmoil is around them, able to stay focused as they choose. As a result they seem more fully there, able to think more clearly and size up both people and situations more accurately. In comparison, others seem to be "not playing with a full deck." In addition to knowing their craft, it is the ability to focus fully in the present that enables Olympic athletes, concert musicians and performance artists to positively use the pressures of the crowds to excel, exceeding their previous bests, and accomplishing peak performance. Active decision-making and problem-solving require *Presence of Mind's* mental clarity to achieve high-quality results, particularly in the midst of stress. To understand *Presence of Mind* even better, let's look at its opposite:

***

MENTAL STRESS

Today most of us are rarely without the mental and emotional challenges of stress. Everyday life now routinely includes tension, racing thoughts, nervousness, anxiety, panic attacks, having too many thoughts at once, feeling overwhelmed, worrying obsessively and "dwelling on problems."

Yet these accepted qualities of modern mental life are not natural. In fact, they are quite unhealthy, too often producing insomnia, concentration loss, and dangerous accidents resulting from distraction and mental overload. (See Figure 5.1) Physical problems such as ulcers, headaches, upset stomachs, high blood pressure, angina attacks and even heart attacks can result from too much worrying. The wear and tear on the body, particularly on the immune system, of constant pessimism, negativity, and a relentless problem-oriented focus can certainly worsen serious illnesses such as cancer, as well as most autoimmune disorders.

Mental Activity During Stress

When we do find ourselves in genuinely life-threatening situations - as with a <u>real</u> saber-toothed tiger - it's perfectly natural for our mental activity to speed up. Our fight/flight response automatically lets us know something is wrong. We then react to identify the danger, and focus on an escape route.

MEMORY AND PRESENCE OF MIND

Internal focus fills conscious attention capacity.

Time focus is in the past, distracting awareness from in the present.

Diminished perception in the present results in impoverished memory.

Fig. 5.1

However, in a modern stress situation, it's not necessarily accurate to automatically assume something is <u>wrong</u>. It's just that something has <u>changed</u>. Yet our survival conditioning positions us to treat almost all change as threatening - and today most of us face a barrage of "change" by simply walking to the corner of the block to mail a letter! When we misinterpret change as danger, our mental activity speeds up to carry out its immediate search-and-find mode for the potentially life-threatening trigger. We look <u>outside</u> to find something wrong.

But like Nasrudin's search <u>outside</u> his home for his key, we may not find what triggered our stress. However, we often begin interpreting many other things negatively, seeing them as problems simply because we are feeling physically uncomfortable. It's like deciding to look around you for the color red. Everything red suddenly jumps out in a visual sense. The mental result? We find lots of things that <u>seem</u> wrong.

Our anxiety and confusion are often increased <u>because</u> there is usually no identifiable physical threat to our lives. We keep looking for "what's wrong," yet our signal of *Change Awareness* is creating the discomforts of stress simply to grab our attention. However, unbeknownst to our automatic survival reaction and to our conscious mind, **that stress trigger now is most often internal and mental, not external and physical.** Much of present day anxiety and catastrophizing comes from this misunderstanding of how we perceive change. Nonetheless, we tax our mental processes trying to sort out the stress signals.

Why Our Minds Race Under Pressure

As a mechanical event, racing thoughts are unaware that the source of most stress is the result of the control "Center" of our unconscious mind, **our intuition**, trying to communicate an important message to our conscious mind: "something is changing!" When that message goes unrecognized - when we don't "pick up the phone" of our intuition - we try to continue thinking the same thoughts we were thinking before the fight/flight response was triggered. The nagging discomforts of stress set in. This now takes us out of the present moment.

Mechanically, we simply exceed our attention capacity's structural limitations and overload it with too many thoughts at once. The thoughts we were thinking before we became stressed are added to the more pressing process of searching for a threat to our lives. However, our conscious attention capacity is limited to focusing on only around <u>seven things at once</u>, plus or minus two, with <u>only one thing in depth at a time</u>.[3]

Going to even 10 things at once yields a...

***

MECHANICAL OVERLOAD!

We cannot hold all these extra thoughts in our mind at once. Yet we insist on trying to do so. Hence our perceptual style shifts, and we "go sequential." We try to recapture the fuller focus of handling all our thoughts at once by <u>mentally speeding up</u>. But we can only approximate and imitate that larger breadth of perception by focusing on everything in a rapid, back and forth, sequential manner.

"Going sequential" is like trying to maintain eye contact while conversing with several people at the same time. When we're talking with just one person, steady eye contact is achievable, though quite challenging at times. If we try to maintain continuous eye contact with two people at once, the tendency is to go from one person's eyes to the other's so quickly that it seems we're covering both people at the same time. If we increase the number of people to eight, suddenly the pace becomes frantic - the speed of our mental activity must increase beyond any comfortable level.

If we persisted in trying to maintain eye contact with all eight people, we'd probably go bonkers rather rapidly, developing eye strain, dizziness, fatigue and whiplash. Having once entered into that racing mode, focusing with clarity and detail on a single set of eyes becomes impossible, because we're still trying to see them all at once.

Review the chart below and check off all the signs of mental stress you have experienced, whether regularly or rarely.

YOUR CHANGE AWARENESS SIGNALS

Focusing **S**ystem

Changes in your mental activity or emotional state:

Racing thoughts	*Fear*
Too many thoughts	*Insomnia*
Concentration loss	*Dwelling on problems*
Constant worrying	*Impatience*
Nervousness	*Negativity*
Anxiety, panic	*Frustration*
Anger, irritation	*Easily distracted*

Fig. 5.2

Awesome, isn't it? We put up with these mental problems because we don't know how to stop them. We live with having to take enormous amounts of tranquilizers, sleeping pills, antacids, muscle relaxers and antidepressants simply because we don't know how to stop thinking. It's as if our mind has left our control and is doing its own thing, whether we like it or not. And many of us do it all the time!

Racing thoughts of worry, anxiety and panic result when we use a sequential perceptual style for accomplishing a more simultaneous and wholistic endeavor. The way out is to shut off the sequential, analytic style of actively thinking by switching into the fuller, more expansive style of passively receiving sensory information which is more relevant for the job. In other words, we focus on:

KEY GOAL

HEAR
all sounds
going on around
you to clear
your mind

Fig. 5.3

Shutting off the sequential mode of thought is easily achieved by establishing *Presence of Mind*. What we call "thinking" is the mechanical activity of paying attention to our internal sensory events - talking to ourselves and looking at the pictures inside our minds. Since <u>we cannot perceive both internally and externally with clarity of focus in any one sense at the same moment</u>, we can establish our perception fully in the present by directing our focus to external events, to noting <u>what is occurring AS it is happening</u>. This is known as **passive perception**, because we are receiving the sensory stimuli that are ongoing in our external environment, without trying to actively change what we're sensing.

In the eye contact situation, we can accomplish this by looking at the center person's forehead, relaxing our eyes and becoming aware of the larger visual field by using our peripheral vision. Precise detail of perception is traded for breadth of perception. The same principle applies to attaining *Presence of Mind*.

Presence of Mind is very easy to generate whenever we want. All we need is the *Presence of Mind* to remember to perform a single basic step. Fortunately, *Presence of Mind* generates *Presence of Mind*, so...

THE MORE WE BECOME AWARE...
THE MORE AWARE WE BECOME.

To achieve peace of mind, we rely on turning on the calming system in the brain. By practicing the exercises at the beginning of this chapter, you will master the essentials of sensory attention-focusing, locating your control levers so you can...

Leave Your Mind And Come To Your Senses.

It's often true that being the most aware and alert person in a room may be more valuable than being the smartest or most educated. Sometimes we find ourselves out in public, in a meeting or someplace where closing our eyes is impractical, and yet we want to invoke *Presence of Mind*. There's a fast, extremely efficient way to clear the mind and focus more fully in the moment.

To gain mental clarity and the greater sensory awareness of *Presence of Mind*, try this:

Step 1. **Focus your gaze on a <u>single</u> object or spot in your external visual field.** A clock, the edge of your desk, a point on the wall, whatever.

PREFERRED FOCUSING SENSE

external

This serves to keep your eyes from moving around - necessary because when your eyes are moving, you're usually actively thinking. "Thinking" is precisely the type of inner dialogue we now wish to silence. Focusing on a spot prevents our normal thought processes and mental activities from being stimulated through our eye movements.

Step 2. **Focus your full attention on listening in the auditory external mode for the next <u>10</u> seconds, <u>naming</u> to yourself each and every sound AS you are hearing it.**

Notice how your consciousness immediately changes from "thinking" to simply "perceiving" the sounds going on around you. Sense how your contact with reality increases instantly, allowing you to feel more "tuned in" to your surroundings. Choosing to mechanically focus externally seems to flood the auditory nerve pathways with outside sounds, simultaneously shutting off our inner chatter, which is auditory in nature.

THIS IS HOW YOU CLEAR YOUR MIND!

Having just cleared your mind, you are now in a great position to refocus your attention fully on whatever you want to pay attention to - YOUR choice. With practice, you can gain *Presence of Mind* within seconds, just by focusing your attention in the auditory external mode.

Again, do yourself a favor. Don't just read about this exercise - do it! You will quickly make a very powerful discovery:

There is no stress in the present.

***

THE TIMING OF STRESS

Stress occurs when we are mentally based in the <u>past</u>, worrying about things that have already happened, or when we are mentally based in the <u>future</u>, anxiously expecting catastrophic events which haven't yet developed.

Presence of Mind **provides us with the timing key for calm.** The more aware we are in any situation, the more capable we are of handling expected and unexpected events. Actually, *Presence of Mind* makes us more capable of handling <u>ourselves</u>, because we can more fully utilize our own knowledge, experience, understanding, intelligence, creativity and wisdom as needed.

Presence of Mind is developed through <u>not</u> doing the things we usually do with our minds. People endowed with *Presence of Mind* are not constantly interpreting, judging and analyzing what's going on. In other words, they are not "thinking." They are perceiving.

"Thinking" is a type of mental activity that actually diminishes *Presence of Mind*. "Thinking" in the way people usually do is what produces stress.

"Thinking" is an active use of our mental processes in which we are directing our thoughts and our attention-focusing into analyzing, describing, dissecting and sequencing our mental stimuli according to our <u>own</u> forms of logic.

"Perceiving" is a more passive receiving of sensory information through our five senses AS the information presents itself to our senses - whether it comes from within us or is external to us. **Through experience, we come to know the difference between thinking and perceiving. This is what gives us the ability to...**

***

BE FULLY PRESENT.

We hear that "timing is everything." This is certainly true with **Presence of Mind**. Because our conscious attention capacity is so limited, it gets quickly filled with thinking about the past or future.

Our challenge is to think WHILE staying aware of the present.

Most folks mentally live in the past, worrying about and regretting things that have already happened - or in the future, anxiously awaiting catastrophes yet to come. This mental orientation is the source of much unnecessary discomfort. It is also unnatural because as human beings **our existential home base is in the present.**

We are correctly called human "beings" - a present tense description. We are not human "was'es" or human "will be's." Many cultures have extraordinary and rich stories about being fully present. One of my favorites comes from the Zen tradition:

> A man was standing on the edge of a steep cliff enjoying the panoramic view. Suddenly the ground he was standing on gave way, and he found himself falling over the edge. On the way down, he managed to grab some branches sticking out of the cliff wall. Having stopped his fall, he surveyed where he was. Looking down, he could see jagged rocks hundreds of feet directly below him. Looking up, he noticed two lions watching him from the top of the cliff where he had been standing. Then he felt the branch that was supporting him starting to pull out of the wall from his weight.
>
> At that moment he saw a patch of wild strawberries growing out of the cliff about a foot away from him.

Holding on to the loosening branch with one hand, he reached over and grabbed a wild strawberry and put it in his mouth. He exclaimed: "How sweet this tastes!"

<u>That's</u> being fully in the present. That is the timing of calm.

Eating strawberries while hanging from a steep cliff wall is a somewhat extreme example of the value of ***Presence of Mind***. Nevertheless, that imperiled berry-eater was adept at gaining...

THE BENEFITS OF PRESENCE OF MIND

Better Memory   *Mental Clarity*

Relief From Insomnia   *Enhanced Sensuality*

Stronger Concentration   *Emotional Neutrality*

Enhanced Ability to Learn   *Greater Contact with Reality*

Greater Sense of Being Alive   *Increased Sensory Awareness*

Fig. 5.4

The calm mind is clear of the distractions of racing thoughts, anxiety, panic, worry and all of the problems associated with mental stress. Clearing the mind gives us back our **full capacity to pay attention** to whatever we want. We can choose both what we want to think about, and what we don't want to think about. This benefits most people who are at the mercy of whatever thoughts come into their minds and can't stop thinking or worrying.

Insomnia is usually experienced as a state in which the body is tired and the mind won't stop thinking. This is why clearing the mind often **remedies insomnia**, especially when combined with the Deep "Sigh" Breaths and passive muscle relaxation. We can consciously calm our three major body systems and make our bodies enter sleep, just by letting go with our muscles more and more - especially our facial muscles - each time we exhale and as we rest, while focusing in the auditory external sensory mode - naming sounds as we hear them. We simply fill our attention capacity with the emotionally neutral content of these activities.

Mental clarity greatly enhances our ability to **concentrate and to learn**. People under stress often have difficulty learning and remembering because their limited attention capacity was filled with the thoughts of the past or the future. Too little of their focus was in the present. We can absorb more and focus more strongly when we are free of the mental distractions that compete for our limited attention capacity. Our ability to **access our memories** is more efficient when our minds are clear. Remembering is a passive receiving of inner images, sounds, words and feelings. The calm, clear mind opens up our inner focus, and in this way also **strengthens our intuition, creativity and our inner guidance**.

MEMORY AND PRESENCE OF MIND

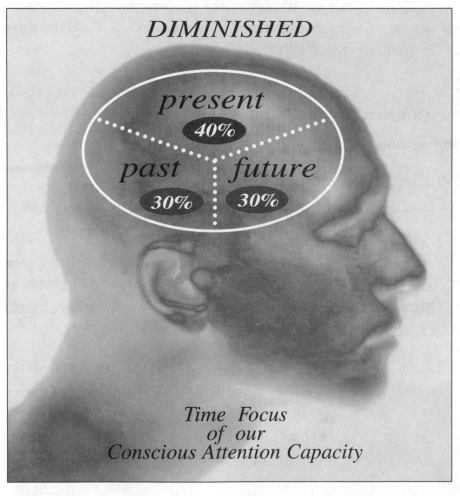

DIMINISHED

present
40%

past   *future*
30%   **30%**

*Time Focus
of our
Conscious Attention Capacity*

*A focus which is 30% filled with concerns, regrets and thoughts of the past, and 30% filled with worries and anxieties about the future, leaves only 40% of our attention capacity to perceive what's going on in our present situation. This diminished perception prevents a strong memory, since we "weren't all there."
Accidents, judgment errors and poor decision-making result from this "distracted" present focus.*

Fig. 5.5

Mental clarity **improves our memory** as well, because we are more present to fully experience our life situations as they are happening, so we naturally remember more. How can we recall what happened if we weren't really "there"? (See Figure 5.5) When we are fully present, we are much more aware of what's going on around us. With *Presence of Mind*, our sense of connection with our external physical reality is enhanced. It's as if **we are in greater contact with reality**.

Whenever you lose that feeling of being in greater contact with reality, you can immediately restore it by...

***

REVVING UP YOUR SENSES
TO FEEL MORE ALIVE

Feeling more and more alive, simply by letting our attention fill with the perceptions our senses are bringing to us, is like sensualizing ourselves. All we need to do is to turn on <u>all three external senses at the same time</u>. It works like this:

- **Focus** in the kinesthetic external sense, **feeling** all the sensations touching your skin over your whole body at once.

- Keep that kinesthetic external focus, and **add** to it the auditory

PREFERRED FOCUSING SENSE

external

external focus, by **listening** to all the sounds going on around you AS they are happening.

- Staying focused in **those two senses**, now **add** to them your visual external sense - by opening your eyes and noticing everything you are **seeing** - while you are hearing and feeling...

- **Focus in all three external senses at the same time....**

- **Enjoy hanging out in this state for the next 2 to 3 minutes.**

Feel how much more alert, aware and alive you now are. Make this a habit when walking to your car, when sitting in a chair, when going for a walk or run, instead of smoking a cigarette or overeating. Nourish yourself with this greater sensory awareness. **Feel how sensual and how alive you can feel through your senses.** (See Figure 5.6)

***

ENJOYING EMOTIONAL NEUTRALITY

One great benefit of *Presence of Mind* is calming our emotions. By focusing in a nonjudgmental manner, like an objective reporter, we feel as if we have neither big emotions going on, nor little emotions. People often describe it as feeling as if their emotions were put in neutral gear. This is a very healthy option to have; we don't need to have our stress emotions going <u>all</u> the time.

MEMORY AND PRESENCE OF MIND

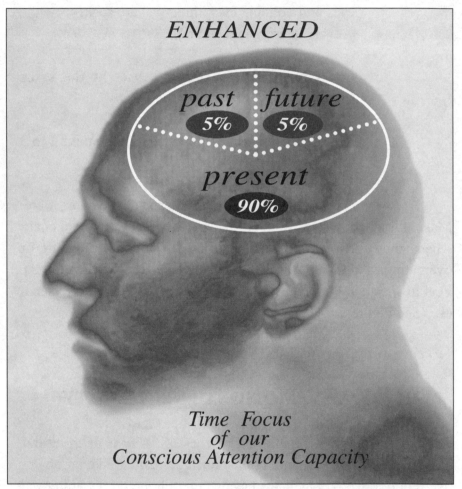

Fig. 5.6

More complete memory, stronger concentration, greater sensory awareness and an enhanced sense of aliveness often result from being more fully focused in the present. Referred to as being "centered" or "grounded," fuller presence of mind allows relevant learnings from the past as well as creative insights to be accessed more easily. Progress toward goals can also be monitored and updated more readily.

Interestingly, many people feel very soothed and peaceful, as if quieting the stress emotions and feeling the peacefulness of the present is, by itself, a natural source of joy. Feeling emotionally neutral helps us to stay focused on the job, despite whatever personal difficulties are going on in our lives. Putting our emotions in neutral through *Presence of Mind* gives us great emotional control, because it enables us to choose what we want to focus our attention on, and not simply be at the mercy of whatever worries flash through our minds. Purposefully taking a few moments to recharge by restoring our emotional calm after a rough day at work allows us to better enjoy our personal time, our quality of life, our friends and our families - free of job pressures now of the past.

Having *Presence of Mind* doesn't mean we never feel emotions again. However, it does give us more control in our lives and the ability to be the mature people we aspire to become. Instead of emotionally blowing up and getting upset in an unpleasant situation - although there are times when that is quite appropriate - we can quickly establish ourselves in the present, clear our minds, put our emotions in neutral, and then <u>decide</u> how we want to respond.

This alternative is far superior to simply reacting like automatons to everyone and everything that pushes our buttons. It even has a side effect of making us feel better about ourselves, more mature, more true to who we are, rather than being in the position of regretting what we said and did because we lacked self-control. *Presence of Mind* provides us with a lifelong skill - to enjoy growing ourselves in the ways <u>we</u> want. Practicing the tools for achieving *Presence of Mind* will remind us that...

We are our most vitalized when we're fully present.

We so enjoy activities that force us into the present - making love, parachuting, being in nature, dancing, downhill racing, listening to a jazz performance - because we feel more alive. They turn us on! With the skills for *Presence of Mind*, we gain this extra aliveness by souping up our senses whenever we want, even in daily mundane activities - and without needing drugs.

You are now well on your way to learning the skills of **TRUE CALM**, and only inches away from mastering the six-second skill of *instant calm*. Before we reach the final lessons **- and while you are continuing to practice! -** we'll explore a fascinating practical use of *Presence of Mind*: how to increase your intuition. Did you know you also have a built-in guidance system that is showing you the way for a happier, more peaceful, more fulfilling existence? In the meantime...

Enjoy your present!

YOUR SIXTH SENSE

"The best player of the game is the watcher - ask him."   Proverb[1]

W e humans come equipped with a fascinating intuitive "sixth sense." "In-tuition" literally means inner tuition or internal teaching. What is that something which is doing the teaching? This is one of the great mysteries of our human experience, and the potential source of our greatest joy.

INTUITION: Our Awareness Of Change

Our sixth sense is constantly tuned into "change," constantly directing us to recognize change, to become more aware of change, and ultimately to change ourselves. Difference is what our sixth sense seeks, and each of our five senses is designed to recognize difference - when something just started, stopped, slowed, shifted, moved, speeded up, got warmer, cooler, wetter, heavier, lighter, brighter, darker, greener, bluer, louder, quieter, saltier, sweeter, more fragrant, stinkier and more interesting.

As our sixth sense <u>senses</u> change, it then signals us to wake up and become aware so we can identify - with our conscious mind and through our five senses - exactly what *is* changing.

Our sixth sense does more than simply compare and

analyze. It has a nose for immediacy. It alerts us instantly WHEN something is changing, telling us that difference is happening **NOW**. So one aspect of this sixth sense is really a sense of timing. It grabs our attention and locks our focus right in the moment, immediately giving us the timing of *Presence of Mind*. However, our ability to "think" has become so overdeveloped that we can ignore this natural instinct and not become more aware of what's going on around us.

One aspect of our intuitive sixth sense of *Change Awareness* is an essential part of our ancient physiological survival mechanism, the "fight/flight emergency response." Remember the urge to look up when we sensed the presence of a saber-toothed tiger? It is as if at an earlier time in the prehistory of our species, "difference" - any difference - was a threat to our very existence. It seems that our physical survival was originally so tenuous that any newness or unfamiliarity presented unexpected danger - and prob-ably did so more often than it presented joy, happiness, security and pleasure. This is likely to be the true physiological root of the prej-udices, bigotries, fears, hatreds and suspicions which prevent us from fully enjoying the wondrous variety of our human colors and cultures.

As we have evolved more fully into our current mental realm, having accomplished basic survival by controlling much of our physical environment, we have nearly lost touch with our own natural intuition. We now need our sixth sense of *Change Awareness*, perhaps more than ever. Rapidly accelerating global, economic, environmental and societal change requires that we now embrace what is our nature, our intuitive sixth sense. We must not merely survive, but *THRIVE* with these enormous changes.

Change Awareness, one aspect of our intuitive sixth sense, is our guidance system for *THRIVING* with rapid global change.

The following exercise will increase your skill in accessing the wisdom of your unconscious mind. It will begin to familiarize you with some of the forms your intuition uses to communicate with you, and should assist you in the task of:

***

LOCATING YOUR SIXTH SENSE

While we can certainly receive intuitive messages in all of our senses, in general we each seem to have a specific sense through which our own intuition mainly works. To determine **your** main intuitive channel, do the following:

Step 1. Think of three situations in which you somehow knew how things were going to turn out before they actually happened, <u>and you were right</u>.

Step 2. Remember back to the actual moment when you suddenly <u>knew</u> and identify in each situation precisely HOW you knew. In other words:

- Did you hear an inner voice telling you? If so, then your intuition communicated via your **auditory internal** sensory mode.

- Did you see what would occur in the situation? If so, then your intuition communicated via your **visual internal** sensory mode.

- Did you get a feeling or a hunch about the situation? If so, then your intuition operated via your **kinesthetic** sensory mode.

- Did you get a funny taste in your mouth? This indicates the **gustatory** sense.

- Did the situation stink? Did it smell like roses or make your nostrils flare? This indicates the **olfactory** sense, your sense of smell.

Step 3. Did each situation use the same sense, or were more than one sense used? If you're not yet certain, then remain curious and notice in the moment which sense(s) you are using to "know" when you're "on."

Use the self-knowledge gained from this exercise to sharpen your awareness, so you can increasingly catch **your** valuable intuitive messages as soon as they occur. Begin to notice the differences between when your intuition is **"on"** with accuracy, and when it's not as sharp.

To engage more fully in dialogue with your unconscious mind and its intuitive guidance, it may help to have a deeper understanding of exactly how it interacts with your everyday, "conscious" mind. Sometimes it's as easy as picking up the phone.

***

THE INTUITION PROCESS
The Call... The Receiver... The Caller

Our inner communication works very much as if we have a telephone system built inside of us. For us to pick up the telephone, we first need to know <u>when</u> it is ringing.

The Call - First Stage Alert: Creative Intuition

We are sensual creatures, and our intuition often communicates through our physical senses. Because our intuition's communications come from outside of our conscious mind's narrow focus, we're surprised when we suddenly have a thought that comes from "out of the blue," from "left field," or from "who knows where." We sense fleeting internal visual images that present us with the perfect creative solution, the right understanding, a new artistic design; then they're gone. We hear a "small, quiet voice within" telling us ever so softly just what we need to know or do; then it's gone. Sometimes we get a feeling about someone, a "gut feeling" that is amazing in its accuracy. Then it's gone.

This is the first stage alert, the famous "first impression" brought directly to us by our intuitive "CENTER," which is *The Caller*. Our challenge is to recognize the differences between these special messages and our normal everyday thoughts.

For example, we know our internal dialogue can range from strategic planning and active rehearsing to constructive debating. It can also become "stuck" dwelling on inane thoughts and meaningless inner chatter, relentlessly worrying, or just not being able to stop hearing a certain song in our minds. However, our inner dialogue also includes an intuitive or higher aspect, a wonderfully insightful inner voice which is wise in the ways of guiding us to act in our own best interests.

Our internal visual sense ranges from pictures of our fantasies, joys, successes and happiest memories to scenes of sorrow, criticism and fear which keep reminding us of disappointments and traumas in our past. But at the more intuitive or higher end of our internal visual sensations, we experience "seeing the big picture," magical moments of creative insight that inspire new approaches to familiar situations, unique solutions, and artistic creations which expand our horizons. Sometimes symbolic images flow into our consciousness, full of profound meaning.

These internal visual and auditory sensations are well acknowledged. Yet our third major sense, the kinesthetic sense or "feeling" sense, also has a wide range. It is in this sense that we can experience quite amazing growth, for this underexplored sense of feeling is possibly the most important one we have for evolving further.

In the familiar range of internal events, we can feel everything from an upset stomach to sexual arousal, from nervousness to joy and expectation. More basic sensations include simply feeling hungry, thirsty, sleepy, lonely or loved. Yet, we also can feel things which have different meaning, like that funny feeling in the pit of our stomach that tells us to be on guard with someone, or the warm feeling that tells us to trust our gut and "go for it" in another situation. Curiously:

Our bodies, and our stomachs in particular, often seem to clearly know things long <u>before</u> our conscious minds do.

At these times, the words we hear, the pictures we see, and the feelings we sense <u>inside</u> contain very important communications about <u>what is changing</u>. To receive that content, we need to perceive those messages **as** they are "happening." This requires having *Presence of Mind - Treasured Quality #3*, in order to focus our attention internally, as we have explored in Chapter Five.

The Call - Second State Alert: STRESS

A most interesting thing follows these intuitions, these early warnings and inner guidances: *when we don't listen, when we don't get the picture, when we don't value the feeling, we experience STRESS.* Why? Because...

STRESS IS NO RANDOM EVENT IN THE BODY.

Stress is a signal that our intuition is calling. Using our bodies as the telephone bell, it is communicating *an awareness of change* to our conscious minds. Our incredible inner wisdom, having been ignored or undervalued, becomes determined to grab the attention of our conscious mind - and it will stop at nothing. If we miss the first stage alert of *Change Awareness*, the signal becomes more intense, louder, more noticeable.

YOUR INTUITION WILL BE HEARD - ONE WAY OR ANOTHER!

Why? Because something just changed and <u>we need to know what it is</u>. Part of our ancient survival mechanism, and now central to our current need to *THRIVE* with rapid global change, our intuition is totally on our side, acting in our best interest. AND... it won't quit.

Instead of benefiting through listening, and ***THRIVING*** with change, too often we treat benevolent communication from our sixth sense as if it is a collect, long-distance, obscene phone call from someone we've never met. Our responses tend to be:

> "Sorry, I don't accept collect charges."
> "You must have a wrong number."
> "Definitely a bad connection."
> "Busy signal, please try your call again."
> "I'm not in, please leave a message at the sound of th upset stomach."
> "Sorry, you have reached a number that isn't in service at this time."

In turn, your intuitive ***Change Awareness*** messenger reacts much as you might in the same situation. If you are trying to deliver an important communication by phone to someone you care about who doesn't answer, you call again. Then you go visit, and knock on the door - loudly. Finally, <u>you break down the door</u>!

The "ignorance" of ignoring our own *Change Awareness* signals carries a heavy price that results in destructive stress - herein defined as "ineffective, unhealthy reactions to change." The constant energy being expended to get our attention and the increased energy exerted resisting the message produce an inner imbalance, the experience of internal conflict which we refer to as "stress." If unresolved over time, the result can be rapid aging of the inner organs and a weakened immune system.

It is most important to understand that when we don't pay attention to these internal messages from ***The Caller***, <u>the signal intensifies as stress</u>, becoming so loud and so uncomfortable that we absolutely **must** pay attention. This is why taking medications, drugs and alcohol to "relieve the "symptoms" of stress is often counterproductive. They numb the signals and mask the message so that its intensity or volume must increase even more! By that time, the signal is often too distorted to be interpreted. If we continue not picking up the phone, our health can become so impaired that all we can focus on is stopping the "phone" from ringing. The signaling itself has become a life-threatening health crisis! (See Figure 6.1)

The rapid heart beat becomes arrhythmia. The stomach gurgling becomes ulcers. The tense muscles become headaches, neck pain, uptight shoulders, lower back pain, pinched nerves. The racing thoughts become insomnia, anxiety and panic attacks. The mental distraction becomes an inability to concentrate, chronic worrying, depression. The increased blood sugar becomes diabetes or hypoglycemia. The pounding heartbeat becomes chronically elevated blood pressure, essential hypertension, heart attacks, strokes. Health and well-being deteriorate.

The curious thing is how **each stress, difficulty and illness conveys a purposeful communication**. For example, a physician friend of mine once told me that in virtually every case of heart attack, the "victim" could remember in hindsight having had various warnings in the form of different sensations and unfamiliar feelings up to <u>nine</u> months before the actual attack. In each case they didn't pay attention to these signals.[2] They just didn't know that the feelings were signals with important meaning for them. Those signals were all saying one thing:

***

PICK UP THE PHONE!!

CHANGE AWARENESS SIGNAL

The Call - *Change Awareness signals through stomach upset.*

Unhealthy Attention-Focusing - *Not answering* **The Call** *only makes the signal increase as "stress" to get our attention.*

Fig. 6.1

Picking up the phone simply means to recognize quickly that the bodily discomforts of stress are valuable signals of communication from *The Caller*, which, as we shall see, is the control "CENTER" of our unconscious mind. Picking up the phone lets *The Caller* know that it has your conscious attention, so it can stop the phone from ringing further. **When the so-called stress has served its communication function properly, its job is done. The stress then stops and dissolves - naturally.** Now *The Caller* can begin transmitting the actual message to...

The Receiver

The Receiver is none other than our conscious mind, which is mechanically limited in its ability to focus. Hence, we must disconnect our focus from whatever we were paying attention to when we received our *Change Awareness* signal, and redirect our attention in the present in two ways: first externally, to make certain there is no physical threat present, and then internally, to get the actual content of our inner guidance.

In other words, we need to know when our *Change Awareness* signal is telling us to change our awareness - from whatever we were focusing on, to what is changing in the present moment.

Healthy *attention-focusing* means knowing *when* our CENTER is calling our conscious mind, and then focusing internally to gain its actual message.

The "stress" nearly always dissolves as soon as we receive its valuable message and act on it. Ironically, this may be precisely the moment when our "ego" - the control center of our conscious mind - stubbornly asserts itself. It often resists change by refusing to acknowledge that an important intuitive message is coming through from an inner part of us that is actually in charge, that knows more than it does.

"If the scissors are not used daily on the beard, it will not be long before the beard is, by its luxuriant growth, pretending to be the head".
Hakim Jami in *The Way of the Sufi* by Idries Shah

The practical question is: "How can we better operate our inner phone system and benefit from the wisdom of *The Caller*?"

CHANGE YOUR AWARENESS TO GET THE MESSAGE

How do we know that stress ends when the conscious mind becomes receptive to messages from the intuitive *Caller*? Some of the evidence can be discerned by examining the very interesting experience which occurs during the first stage alert of *The Call*.

This experience has been described within a well-documented therapeutic technique called "Focusing" (a process culled from studying clients who successfully adapted to change). From "Focusing" comes the concept of "body shift."[3] This is a feeling of release, of relief, of flowing - of a blockage being removed. What produces this release, by all accounts, is the simple process of accurately matching the body signal (the **feeling** of stress or discomfort) with the internal words and/or images associated with it - so the conscious mind makes the connection between the two. In other words...

COMMUNICATING THE MESSAGE
IS ACCOMPLISHED!

There is no further need for the body to transmit signals. The conscious mind can now interpret and understand the meaning of the body feelings by knowing the internal words and visual images that go with these body signals. The emotional and physiological components of the release caused by making this internal match have not been thoroughly investigated by researchers for their health effects, but we can infer from the patients' verbal descriptions citing relief of discomfort, from their lack of development of further illness, and from their ability to move on with life, that something **very healthy** is accomplished!

It's as if the sole intention of the unconscious behavior is to achieve communication. That's all. There's no judgment, no self blame, no ridicule, no punishment - nothing but an accurate communication. **Receiving the communication from our intuitive CENTER is often all that is desired by the unconscious mind.** This liberating and exhilarating psychological discovery means that the unconscious mind is benevolent after all. It means that the answers to our emotional discomforts, stresses, anxieties, and personal difficulties are indeed within us - and can be acquired in a very practical manner. The main reason we haven't become proficient at perceiving our intuitive signals is that we haven't known that emotions, bodily sensations, internal images, words and external events can actually be communications. Picking up the phone and getting the message from *The Caller* is how we improve our health, relieve stress, develop greater self-confidence, raise self-esteem and cultivate greater intuition.

This we call "self-knowledge." The goal is simply to be aware of one's own inner experience. And that involves knowing <u>when</u> and <u>how</u> to pick up the phone, which is the same as recognizing...

***

YOUR *CHANGE AWARENESS* SIGNALS

Our goal is to open up the communication pathways between the grander knowing of our perceptive, intuitive CENTER and our conscious mind so we can reap the benefits of its wisdom. With respect to human evolution, accomplishing this goal surpasses the importance of putting the first human on the moon. **Moving our conscious awareness into our intuitive CENTER is our next evolutionary step. The state of TRUE CALM, with its *Four Treasured Qualities* operating together at the same time, accelerates our access.**

"When the snake has straightened itself, it enters the hole." Proverb
Dermis Probe by Idries Shah

On a practical level, feeling calm and stopping the fight/flight emergency response whenever you want are part of this growth process. Read through the following list of common stress signals. Circle each body signal of stress that you have experienced or are experiencing in stressful situations. These are the ways YOUR *Caller* is attempting to contact your conscious mind, *The Receiver*, through your body.

YOUR CHANGE AWARENESS SIGNALS

Muscle System

Tensed, cramped or tight muscles in these body areas:

Forehead   Shoulders
Temples   Chest tightness
Eyes   Stomach knots
Clenched jaw   Lower back
Teeth grinding   Thighs
Neck/throat   Calves
Arms/hands   Feet, toes

Breathing System

Changes in the activity of your internal organs:

Adrenaline rush   Stomach upset
Heart racing   Intense headache
Pounding pulse   Appetite gain or loss
Perspiration   Dry mouth
Rapid, shallow breath   Stomach butterflies
Cold hands or feet   Dizzy
Face flushing   Light-headed

Focusing System

Changes in your mental activity or emotional state:

Racing thoughts   Fear
Too many thoughts   Insomnia
Concentration loss   Dwelling on problems
Constant worrying   Impatience
Nervousness   Negativity
Anxiety, panic   Frustration
Anger, irritation   Easily distracted

Fig. 6.2

Each of these may be a signal from your CENTER to your conscious mind to change your focus of attention from the external to the internal. When you have established that the phone is ringing and have then, in fact, picked up the receiver, you will then soon be able to report that...

***

THE MESSAGE IS RECEIVED

How can we get the message? First things first. Blocking our receiving a clear message is the noisy ringing of *The Call*... the distracting *Change Awareness* signals alerting us through stress: the tense muscles, heart pounding, upset stomach, the racing thoughts, panic and so on. These distractions occur because we have missed the first stage alert of our intuition and the second stage alert of stress has followed. **Thus, we generally need to produce calm in addition to picking up the phone.** As you will see, this is easily accomplished by using the six-second skill of *instant calm,* as described in Chapter Ten.

However, even though *instant calm* will stop the stress reactions under virtually any condition, if the communication isn't received and valued enough to be listened to, looked at and felt, then the phone will start ringing again. **More stress will be created no matter how many medications, drinks and drugs are imbibed.** So... in order to save the wear and tear on our bodies, we must pick up the phone immediately. That will be helped by developing...

***

QUICKER INTUITIVE AWARENESS

To improve your skills at recognizing change, and to improve your ability to receive your intuition's messages, note which of your **Change Awareness** signals is the very first one you experience. Number your first three signals. Be aware of them, as if they were, in fact, signals from your internal telephone.

The most useful attitude with which we can approach our inner guidance is one of great curiosity. "What is my intuition trying to tell me?" "What has just changed?" Of course, it helps to know that our CENTER, the source of our intuition, is totally on our side, because it IS us. Our CENTER has our very best interests at heart and is grandly benevolent. If we listen to it, we win. The sooner we get the message, the sooner we reap the rewards and benefit from its greater knowing. Because this signal is coming from our own intuition, we can confidently assume that a larger, wiser part of us <u>already knows</u>. Our conscious mind needs to **Change** its **Awareness** by redirecting its focus in the present to find out what the message is. (See Figure 6.3)

Instant calm achieves this quickly, and will be taught in Chapter Ten. Then we can focus internally to identify **The Call's** actual content. Exactly what words did our inner voice say? What exactly were the details in that inner picture? Just what did we feel about the situation? Like an inner detective game, getting the details is exciting and inspiring because it comes from within ourselves. While we do need to distinguish normal chatter and our wishful thinking (or our fears) from that true voice within, we gain the skill just by the practice of paying attention.

<u>**Now**</u> that you know you have a inner communication system, <u>when</u> the phone is ringing, and <u>how</u> to pick up the phone, you can **gain** the enormous benefits of establishing contact with...

CHANGE AWARENESS SIGNAL

Healthy Attention-Focusing - *We pick up the inner phone by focusing inside to receive the message from our intuitive CENTER.*

Message Received - *Its communication purpose fulfilled, the "stress" dissolves and we THRIVE by correctly using our Change Awareness signal.*

Fig. 6.3

The Caller

The source for the inner sense of guidance we call our intuition or our "sixth sense" is our "unconscious" mind.

The term "unconscious" does not describe the immensity of what this special awareness encompasses. That it is not "conscious" does not mean it is without **awareness, wisdom, organization and purpose.** As those who have attained any degree of self-awareness suspect, and as even the most intellectually driven of us begrudgingly accept, this is the part of us which is actually in charge, not our smaller conscious mind. The unconscious mind, which monitors change, **also has a control center, or "inner ego."** This is the source of our creativity, our intuition and our inner guidance.

For example, while you are reading this sentence, your body is producing 5,000,000 red blood cells and propelling them into your bloodstream each second! The limited conscious mind couldn't stay on top of that task, much less the additional ongoing responsibilities of metabolism, digestion, assimilation, elimination, respiration and so on. The unconscious is also caretaker for the rest of our experience: imaginings, dreams, memories, thoughts, emotions, understandings, creativity, fantasies and the abilities to understand how things are interrelated in larger patterns.

You can see that this awesome part of us is immense in its understanding. In fact, we cannot fit the vast scope of the unconscious mind's capacity into the narrow band of perception we have developed in our conscious mind. Remember, our conscious attention is limited to about seven things at once, and only <u>one</u> of those in real depth at a time. However, being "conscious" of this, we can allow the wisdom and guidance of our unconscious, our CENTER, to filter into our consciousness with more appreciation and greater frequency.

BE CURIOUS - IT'S FUN!

As we practice and gain more experience, an extraordinary development blossoms within us quite naturally. We gain...

SELF-RESPECT, SELF-ESTEEM, SELF-CONFIDENCE & SELF-LOVE

By valuing, perceiving, respecting and acting on these fascinating inner guidances, we literally "grow" our true sense of SELF. When we do, we enter a quite interesting adventure and life becomes much more magical. We all know of occasions when we somehow "knew" something and didn't act on it, only to miss out on a great opportunity. We heard our inner voice, we saw the big picture, or we had a hunch that was right on the money. Later, we remembered having received those communications clearly, and regretted not having trusted them. **This inner trust is the practical foundation of what we call SELF-esteem, SELF-respect, SELF-confidence and SELF-love.**

The ability to listen to our inner guidance improves with practice. Just like building up a big muscle, it becomes easier and easier until we have a direct line of communication between our conscious mind and our intuitive CENTER. Then we have a most amazing inner guidance system to steer us much more smoothly through life's changes. (See Figure 6.4)

Not listening, not respecting, and not benefiting are the practical level behaviors of low self-esteem, low confidence, insecurity, self-doubt and lack of self-love. Striving to gain communications from our CENTER and respecting them by acting on them **IS** the act of self-respect.

DETOUR FOR CHANGE

What tells us when we sense there's change?
We might feel stress or something strange
Lights flash, sounds thump, things jump inside
When what we want and WHAT IS collide.

Then obstacles do block our path
We kick and scream, but cannot laugh
If we instead in the present be
New paths to travel we can see.

Fig. 6.4

135

This is what produces high self-esteem, confidence, security and self-love. These positive, life-enriching qualities are steadily developed by daily attention to your *Caller*, not by pretending to be assured or by hoping to magically overcome years of insecurity. Practice does it.

It's helpful to keep in mind that change is itself neither good nor bad - it simply is always going on. Our reactions to life's changes are what either benefit us, or hurt us. Slowly we have been transforming this knee-jerk survival reaction to change, difference and newness. Today, at least in some life areas, we go so far as to seek out difference and uniqueness. We crave discovering the latest fashion, the look most hip, the newest musical sound, the most technologically innovative audio/video system and who's doing what creative twist in the art world. Change can be inspiring.

TRUE CALM helps us to clean the filters of our perceptual lens so that we can better receive the gifts our intuition provides. And as we do this, our automatic fear-based and anger-based reactions to newness, difference and change in life are replaced with curiosity, alertness, awareness and greater objectivity. In fact, calm promotes greater objectivity, expanded perception and the ability to make the right effort at the right time.

***

Now you have a good idea how your own inner guidance system works. What awaits you are the deeper, grander, most important uses of the **TRUE CALM** skills, beyond merely feeling calm and remedying stress. We need a way to directly connect with *The Caller*, the source of our intuition and creativity. We do this by **feeling** our intuitive CENTER, which is also the source of our...

UPLIFTING ENERGY....

KEY GOAL

RECOGNIZE
your first three
Change Awareness
signals

Fig. 6.5

CHAPTER SEVEN

UPLIFTING ENERGY
Treasured Quality #4

"Sunshine proves its own existence."　Proverb[1]

Welcome to the crown jewel of **TRUE CALM!** You are about to learn how to uplift, invigorate, soothe and refresh yourself whenever you want. *Uplifting Energy* distinguishes **TRUE CALM** from feeling simply relaxed or calm.

Producing the mind/body emotional "state" of **TRUE CALM** with the skills for the *Four Treasured Qualities* gives you an unique evolutionary opportunity. You can now find and open up the faucet of your own *Life Energy*.

When we speak of our *"Life Energy,"* we are talking about our central life force. This energy is at our essence - our core. We all have a source of *Life Energy* within us, energy that is also unique to each of us. Some days we feel "more like ourselves" than other days. When we feel a bit off, we say we're "not ourselves." The difference we are describing is the **feeling** of the force and flow of our *Life Energy*. Is it flowing freely and circulating completely throughout us? Or is it blocked and restricted?

You can enjoy and increase the feeling of your *Life Energy*. You can access and stimulate it - mechanically! - just as you learned to control your breathing, your muscles, and your various internal and external senses. Wouldn't it be great to be able to remove any blockages and feel your life force bathe your muscles, your organs, and your cells in its *uplifting*, healing, life-giving *energy*?

Like everything else in the material plane, we are energy beings or constructs of energy. For example, if we analyze the content of our physical structure, breaking down our muscles and bones into their smaller components, we go from protein materials, to their amino acids, to molecules, to biochemical ingredients and then to their atoms. Going further, each individual atom is made up of electrons, protons, neutrons and even smaller parts **which are all forms of energy.** Even more intriguing is the realization of modern physics that "solid" material objects - such as trees, furniture, concrete and metal - are actually composed of so much space that our entire planet could fit inside a tennis ball by removing the space or energy fields between and within their objects' subatomic particles.[2] Basically, human *Life Energy* is a rich combination of electromagnetic and other energy fields that flow within us, through us, and around us.

The best way to understand your own *Life Energy* is not by thinking, picturing or talking about it. The best way is to:

FEEL YOUR ENERGY!

Sit in a comfortable chair, or stand with your feet placed hip-width apart. Then...

- Place the palms of your hands together in front of you. Press your palms together firmly but lightly, and move one hand in a circular motion. Make quick circles, producing heat from the friction of rubbing your hands together. Count at least 60 circles, moving one hand as quickly as you can while pressing it firmly against your other hand. This takes about one minute. Then...

• Stop rubbing and hold your palms about one inch apart. **Feel** the tingling sensations in your palms and between your hands. Now move one hand in a <u>very slow</u> circle. Keep your palms one inch apart and focus on **feeling a ball of energy between your palms.**

What you feel is your <u>energy field concentrated between your hands</u>. In Russia this is what is called the "bioplasma" energy field.

• Finally, move that energy ball up to your fingertips by looking at and focusing on your fingertips. **Feel** the energy ball move up. Now move that concentrated energy back down to your palms by focusing your eyes on your palms. **Feel** the energy ball move back to your palms.[3]

Interesting, isn't it?

Like electrons orbiting around their nucleus, which itself is filled with neutrons, protons, quarks, "love strings" and other unseen subatomic particles, our energy fields are uniquely related to our core energy. Each of us is composed of fields of energy. In fact, <u>every</u> object and being is an energy field - animals, plants, insects, rocks, even this book, and the chair you're sitting on as you read!

You have just had a direct experience of *feeling your energy* and moving your energy by *focusing your attention*. The "energy ball" exercise plays with a concentration of the energy surrounding your body. You will shortly learn something more valuable: how to generate and circulate energy **inside** your body - an experience you will definitely **want to feel**.

But first, let's explore some of the basics.

***

WHAT IS *LIFE ENERGY*?

Life Energy is not a familiar concept to most people in the cultures of the West, except perhaps as a vague abstraction. However, the older, more continuous cultures of the Pacific, of the Far East and Asia, have long been familiar with *Life Energy* as a concrete, practical instrument for achieving enriched health and greater longevity. They have each named it. In China, as we know, *Life Energy* is called *"chi."* In Japan and Korea, it is *"ki."* Polynesian islanders refer to *Life Energy* as *"ha"* (as in Hawaii), while in India, it is called *"prana."* These cultures have thousands of years of experience in the mechanics of improving and increasing one's *Life Energy*, activities which have been nearly invisible to the average person in the West.

Life Energy is not strictly physical. Having strong *Life Energy* isn't as simple as making sure our bodies house healthy amounts of vitamins and minerals, muscles, protein, fat or stored carbohydrates. *Life Energy* is not the same as enthusiasm, get-up-and-go, or the pep of a cheerleader. It's not an attitude. Nor is strong *Life Energy* simply an emotional experience. It's different from the emotional. It's also different from the psychological. Having strong *Life Energy* doesn't only mean being mentally upbeat, optimistic, and trying to see the good side of every situation. However, the greater flow of our *Life Energy* has positive effects on those realms of experience.

***

LIFE ENERGY AND GREATER HEALTH

Developing our energy fields provides an exciting new frontier for exploring greater health. *Life Energy* is key to developing powerfully hardy immune systems as well as discovering and preventing illness before it has a chance to manifest physically. Using our *Life Energy* to directly improve our health may seem like a new concept, although in fact it is actually thousands of years old. Throughout the ages, healers were those with the ability to generate and impart additional *Life Energy* to the sick.

The modern world is moving into what is called energy medicine. In Western medicine, energy is already being used to diagnose and treat health problems, though in relatively crude ways. The energy-based technologies of X-rays, barium treatments, and CAT scans are regularly incorporated in diagnostic procedures. Ultrasound is used to help accelerate the healing of hard tissues by increasing circulation to ligaments and cartilage, as well as to detect the growth of tumors. MRI's are used for diagnosis in situations of life-and-death, with sometimes hazardous results from bombarding cells with a particular energy vibration that is too powerful. Radiation therapy is also used to stop the growth of cancer cells, even though how and when this successfully works, which isn't often enough, is still a great mystery.

In our culture, natural *Life Energy* is frequently bypassed in favor of the "quick fix." Too often we turn to caffeine and sugar drinks to turbocharge the adrenal glands, forcing them to release their energy hormones: adrenaline and noradrenaline. This quick fix occurs at great cost, for caffeine and sugar bring no vitamins and minerals into the body. Just to process these substances the body has to borrow nutrients, leaving a large nutrient debt in the body. Like most debts, a nutrition debt, if not repaid with proper nourishment, extracts interest. Energy from the adrenal glands is designed for the short term stresses of life-or-death, fight/flight situations. Overusing adrenal energy to meet constant daily events can lead to rapid aging of the internal organs and can weaken immune strength. Overall health is taxed by this energy depleting stress. Shortly, headaches, colds and illnesses such as diabetes, ulcers, heart disease and cancer can more easily begin their march. The quick fix for more energy really means less energy, compromised health - or worse - in the long run.

LIFE ENERGY IS THE SOURCE OF OUR HEALTH

The Chinese view is that the flow of chi, or *Life Energy*, feeds the internal organs, vitalizing them with energy that flows along certain well established pathways, called meridians, which function much like nerve pathways. When an internal organ is diseased or not working properly, it is because its energy supply has become stuck or blocked. The *chi* then needs to be stimulated to increase its life-giving flow to that needy organ. Many ways exist to accomplish this, including acupuncture, acupressure, herbs, exercises and dietary changes. Acupuncture, for example, unblocks, opens and stimulates the *Life Energy* flow by putting very thin needles into the body at certain known points along the energy pathways or meridians. The existence of these points, and of the meridians themselves, has been verified by medical researchers using medical CAT scan equipment in France.[4] Scientists have now verified an additional circulatory system of electrical circuits, whose proper functioning can help explain "miraculous" recoveries from terminal illness.[5]

In China, *Life Energy* is most familiarly produced through the exercises of Tai Chi, and more directly through "Chi Gong," the internal energy techniques. Tai Chi's gentle, flowing movements, designed to give the body an energy tune-up, seem to stimulate the flow of *Life Energy*, while also loosening joints, relaxing muscles, calming the mind, and producing a wonderful sense of peacefulness. Practitioners of Tai Chi have reported rather amazing improvements in their health, including lowered blood pressure and relief from ulcers, arthritis and lower back pain.

We have already explored how to conserve our energy by replacing the qualities of stress with their opposites: *Presence of Mind, Physical Relaxation, and Emotional Peace.* The next step in mastering **TRUE CALM** allows us to access *Uplifting Energy*. It directly rejuvenates and nourishes us by **increasing the soothing flow of our own life force.**

Once again, we accomplish that by focusing our attention internally, now in a kinesthetic or "feeling" mode. It is with joy that I introduce to you a simple, elegant, powerful way to develop, become intimate with, and increase your *Life Energy*. Here is how to **TURN ON**:

***

YOUR LITTLE SUN

This exercise is best done with your eyes closed, as you sit comfortably in a calm, relaxed state. You can either have some-one read the instructions to you very slowly, or tape them to play back to yourself so that you won't be distracted by opening your eyes to read each step.

- **BEGIN BY CALMING YOURSELF** with the basic exercises you have learned so far: the Deep "Sigh" Breath, followed by Small Stomach "Sigh" Breaths. Relax your muscle systems with the release levers you have already prac-ticed. Clear your mind and enjoy the greater

PREFERRED FOCUSING SENSE

internal

sensory awareness exercises you have been learning. Stay alert and fully awake in the present. When you reach the state of calm which is by now becoming very familiar to you, close your eyes and begin the follow-ing exercise:

Step 1. **Picture a Little Sun in the sky a few feet above your head, very bright and shiny**. Your eyes should be closed; you are picturing this Little Sun <u>in your mind's eye</u> and feeling it hov-ering over you. This Little Sun is full of energy, bubbling over with an enormously abundant supply of *Life Energy*. There is no energy crisis here - the Little Sun's energy supply is boundless. It is a joyous, happy Little Sun - untainted by anything mental, emotional, social or political. It <u>is</u> pure *Life Energy*.

Step 2. **Picture a small circle on top of your head, and let the circle expand.** Feel it opening up.

Step 3. **Lower the Little Sun through the circle and bring it into your head,** brightening up your head from the inside. Feel the glow of the Little Sun as its light fills your brain. Continue bringing the Little Sun past your head, into your neck - very bright and shiny. Try to **feel its light.** Now...

Step 4. **Bring the Little Sun past your neck and into your chest area.** Feel where the center of your chest is, inside of you, and take your time feeling that space within. **Let the Little Sun come to rest in the center of your chest area, which is its home. Picture** your Little Sun shining there, very brightly and **feel** the center of your chest area at the same time so that you **connect these two sensations!** Then...

Step 5. **Let the Little Sun's light radiate all throughout your body,** filling you, as if your body is an empty shell, and the light is liquid light. As the Little Sun stays in the center of your chest, its home, let its light radiate out - filling up your head and neck, your shoulders, arms, hands and fingers. **Feel the light** fill up your back, spine, chest and torso, your hips, thighs, knees, calves, feet, and even your toes. **See how brightly your Little Sun can shine.**

Step 6. **Continue picturing your Little Sun radiating and shining its light, filling up your whole body with light.** **FEEL IT** as you picture it. Enjoy how you're feeling, for this is how you begin the wonderful process of generating greater *Life Energy* within yourself.

Memorize this visual process, then turn your attention to the kinesthetic internal sense, so you can focus fully on **FEEL-ING the Little Sun and its light.** You want to do this because, while visualizing is a great tool, the kinesthetic sense is even more important for generating *Life Energy*. Remember:

Feeling is the most direct way to experience your *Life Energy*.

It's wonderful when we sense more *Life Energy* - OUR *Life Energy* - within us. Now - how <u>did</u> you feel during this cozy experience with your Little Sun?

Sometimes people don't feel anything the first few times they practice opening their Little Sun. But just as you felt the energy ball between your hands, you will eventually feel your Little Sun. As you continue practicing, ask yourself...

Did you feel any warmth in your chest area? With practice, your Little Sun will grow brighter and spread even more warmth inside your chest. That warm feeling tells you the general location of your own, unique, internal energy source.

Did you feel any tingling sensations, perhaps in your hands and feet? Great! Those sensations signal that increased *Life Energy* is flowing through its energy pathways in your body. It is as if the denser physical body's resistance to a higher vibratory frequency of energy creates the sensation of tingling.

Finally, did you experience a vibration coming from the Little Sun itself? Did it feel as if you had a little motor inside? Now you're getting somewhere! This <u>is</u> your faucet!

When you locate the source of your own energy, you can tap into it whenever you want, opening this faucet of *Life Energy* to flow freely and powerfully. This feels invigorating and soothing at the same time. And you can make it last as long as you like, just by...

***

KEEPING YOUR ENERGY FAUCET WIDE OPEN

By practicing the Little Sun exercise you will become more adept at keeping your life force flowing. Cultivating the **feeling** sense of the Little Sun helps guide you to feel how to open your internal faucet wider and wider, by letting go. Soon you will be accessing more *Life Energy* with less effort.

To open your "faucet" more and more, concentrate. With your attention focused in the internal feeling sense, you can precisely locate the <u>source</u> of the vibration. This is your energy faucet. When you feel yourself "catch it," you'll get a delightful rush of your own *Life Energy* flowing within you. With continued experience you can open your energy faucet and <u>hold it open</u>. When you achieve this control...

You will be able to lift your spirits whenever you want for the rest of your life!

Of course, mastery comes with practice.

***

YOUR LITTLE SUN WITHIN

Picture your Little Sun, shining brightly above your head.

Bring your Little Sun inside your head and then further inside your body. Feel it as you picture it.

As you picture it, FEEL your Little Sun shining brightly in the center of your chest area, radiating its light throughout your body.

Fig. 7.1

HOW TO PRACTICE

I recommend two ways to practice feeling your Little Sun:

- Daily, and with full concentration, focus for 5 to 6 minutes with the goal of finding and opening the faucet of your *Life Energy* flow.

- Frequently throughout the day, and especially when stressed, quickly picture your Little Sun brightly beaming in the center of your chest area. Feel it. Even 2 seconds is enough! You are opening your energy faucet little by little, more and more. You are evolving yourself energy-wise.

Some people are excellent at visualizing the Little Sun from the start. Being "visual" is very easy and natural to them. If you are one of them, then your challenge is to keep the image of the Little Sun and concentrate on intensely **feeling** the Little Sun's energy.

Many people are slightly frustrated when learning to visualize their Little Sun. You may only see a tiny Little Sun at first, or it may be larger, but not as bright as you may wish. One day you might see a radiant Little Sun, and the next day it may seem less vivid. These variations of experience are quite common early on, a normal part of the learning process. But stick with it! Patience and repeated effort are your friends in energizing yourself. You may be one of the special ones who qualifies as a "fourth horse."

In the Zen tradition, it is said that there are four kinds of horses: excellent ones, good ones, poor ones and bad ones. The best horse will run slow and fast, right and left, at the driver's will, before it sees the shadow of the whip. The good horse will run as well as the first one does, just before the whip touches its skin. The poor horse will run when it feels pain on its body. The fourth horse will run after the pain penetrates to the marrow of its bones. Contrary to our expectations, the fourth horse may be the most valuable, because its struggles to learn give it greater depth and breadth of knowledge.[6]

The *feeling* of *Life Energy* is what you want to cultivate. For some people, this may take only a week, a day, a month of practicing. For others it may take six months to a year of steady practice. But if you persist in this ancient struggle, like the "fourth horse," you will be forever grateful that you did. Your mastery will be more profound, and you will become as perceptive as the "first horse."

You will open your energy faucet.

Nearly everyone who experiences their Little Sun has a different and uniquely personal response. Some people start crying immediately upon putting it in their chest area. But the tears are joyful, like the reunion of two long-lost family members after years of separation. Some people giggle and laugh as a feeling of happiness spreads inside of them. Some people can easily picture the Little Sun above their heads, but seem to lose the image when bringing it into their heads. Some can keep a clear picture of the Little Sun through their head and neck, but not into their chest. Other people get their Little Sun into their chest area, then complain that it seems dark, shadowy, and covered up, not very bright and shiny.

**Difficulty in picturing and feeling the Little Sun is usually
a <u>perfect</u> depiction of the relationship between
that person and their true SELF.**

Difficulty means there's not enough connection with one's SELF, too little love of one's SELF, not enough valuing of one's SELF. The purpose of the difficulty is simply to overcome it.[7] The difficulty is benevolently directing us to make the proper effort we need - not necessarily more effort, just the right effort. As explained earlier, it's like tuning our focus exactly to the right frequency to get a clear radio signal.

In practical terms, a stronger concentration must be made to remove the difficulty. In other words, practice, **focus** on the picture of the Little Sun, and feel it. Keep going for it! This is how we establish the Little Sun solidly within, opening its flow of beautiful *Uplifting Energy* and feeling the gifts of our life force. Yet this inner source is much more grand than we might recognize. As the energy beings that we are, connecting with our core energy supply accomplishes an increasing ability to...

***

SENSE YOUR TRUE SELF.

A major ingredient for feeling calm within yourself is possessing a true sense of SELF. So many people complain that they are full of stress, depressed, pessimistic, imprisoned by their self-critical thoughts, and plagued by their worries, fears and anxieties. Few of us actually have a sense of self in which to feel stable, secure and comfortable - despite <u>whatever</u> changes and difficulties may be going on around us. The Little Sun gives us a practical means of having a sense of self, a way or vehicle for knowing ourselves.

OUR CENTER

The Little Sun is an image that represents our big SELF, our CENTER. Remember, that SELF is not the little self, the conscious analytic mind, the storage place of our conditioning, our self-images and the limitations born from being able to focus on only seven things at once. The control center of that smaller, survival-oriented aspect of our being is commonly referred to as the "ego." The small self is a mechanical accumulation of our joys, pains, successes, failures, pleasures, traumas, dreams, fears, as well as the conclusions we have made about ourselves and about life based on these experiences. Over time we become so familiar with and used to our small self, we end up thinking of ourselves and completely identifying ourselves as this small self. This has been humorously portrayed:

> *"If the scissors are not used daily on the beard, it will not be long before the beard is, by its luxuriant growth, pretending to be the head"*.
>
> Hakim Jami in *The Way of the Sufi* by Idries Shah

While this small self has great value for analyzing, dissecting, describing and thinking, the small self is not the SELF we benefit from by identifying <u>as ourselves</u>. It simply cannot do us justice. This is <u>good</u> news!

Our big SELF is the source of our intuition, our inner guidance and our creativity.

This is the SELF which is actually in charge, despite the wishful thinking of our ego. The understanding, awareness and immense consciousness of our big SELF has been revered throughout the ages by wise people, artists and spiritual leaders. Permanently connecting with this part of us can be considered a description of the goal of the spiritual quest.

The big SELF has been named differently in many spiritual pathways. In Zen, it is called "Big Mind." In Buddhism it is the "Buddha Mind." Christians refer to it as "the Christ Consciousness." In modern spirituality, it is simply called the "Higher Self." In psychology it can be called the "control center of the unconscious mind." Whatever names we call it don't really matter, for it has its <u>own</u> reality. What matters is that it refers to the part of us which is our true SELF, the real us, our essence.

"It" could also be thought of as the center of our soul, the element of God within us. We even use the word "spirit" to describe this non-physical element. What we are actually talking about is something very precious.

***

Often missing from our understanding of ourselves as human beings is that the SELF, the Big Mind or the Higher Self, is not something "out there," but something both in and around us. **We already encompass this grandness, and we can access it within ourselves simply through the sustained effort of focusing our attention in certain ways.** We do need a way to directly connect.

As attention-focusing creatures we need a symbol or image to stabilize our focus. In our physical universe the most powerful image is the sun. It is the essence of all life on our planet. It makes things grow. The sun brings light and warmth, and is a source of enormous, abundant energy. Having a benevolent symbol for this aspect of ourselves - the "Little Sun" - gives us a tremendous advantage in our growth, our creativity and our understanding. By utilizing the symbol of the sun, we are cultivating these qualities within us. (See Figure 7.2)

Dr. Barbara Brown, a psychophysiologist and pioneer in the use of biofeedback for mind/body control, presents evidence for our human ability to evolve new neurological pathways.[8] While this is obvious in the light of long term evolution, where, for example, we have developed our brains in four stages, she suggests that <u>we can choose to evolve or grow new neurological pathways through using our minds consciously</u>. The Little Sun provides a practical example of this.

Since the Little Sun represents our CENTER, the source of our intuition, creativity and inner guidance, the immense wisdom of this inner SELF becomes much more accessible to our conscious mind when we focus on this symbol. It is literally like growing new neurological pathways that open up the greater perspective of our unconscious mind to our smaller conscious mind. That is, being focusing creatures, we can literally "grow ourselves"[9] in new ways by focusing on the symbol which represents our higher big SELF!

The natural result is that gradually we are better able to recognize patterns in how things work, and how things interact as part of larger systems.

YOUR LITTLE SUN ENGINE

Adrenal glands designed for less
Than constant wear and tear of stress
They energize short term it's true
For life/death change: fight/flight, then through.

Overtaxed, fast organ-aging
Immune strength weakens, not behaving
A different source is what we need
For energy from which to feed.

The Little Sun is quite a jewel
When it comes to healthy fuel
Life Energy, so grand a gift
Provides a constant, smooth uplift.

Fig. 7.2

This is the prized ability to "see the big picture." This is the wonderfully exciting "ah hah!" experience of suddenly understanding whatever was once puzzling to us. We become wiser, more creative, and more in touch with our intuition. We become connected with our SELF.

On a practical level, we can better receive the important communications of **Change Awareness** from our intuition and inner guidance. A joyous dimension is added to our relationship with ourselves. A fascinating bit of mystery and adventure enlivens our daily, mundane conscious thought as these intuitive insights increasingly enter our awareness. The Little Sun is an eminently practical vehicle for fulfilling our potential.

Techniques for generating **Life Energy** have not, until now, been widely known. They require patience, continuous effort, and determination. The Little Sun works - guaranteed. It is up to you to make it work for you. All you need to do is make a sustained effort, optimally on a daily basis, to focus your attention internally until you achieve it.

However, once you get your Little Sun open so you can feel its invigorating, *uplifting*, and soothing *energy*, you can invoke it easily and quickly wherever you choose. In fact...

YOU CAN KEEP IT TURNED ON ALL THE TIME!

This may take a week, six months or six years. But however long it takes, you are accumulating enormous benefits along the way. It is something to continue doing daily for a lifetime.

What a gift to yourself, and to all around you, when your Little Sun is beaming within! While the tingling of energy you felt from rubbing your palms together was interesting, and probably pleasant as well, having this powerful energy source vibrating <u>inside</u> of your chest area boosts your emotions, raises your spirits, strengthens your immune system, and opens up neurological pathways to the source of your creativity, intuition, and inner wisdom.

The result is a wiser, calmer, happier, more confident and more creative human being - YOU. The Little Sun makes it possible - mechanically - to feel good inside nearly all of the time. This is why...

You WANT to TURN ON your LITTLE SUN.

***

You are well on your way to becoming adept at the *Four Treasured Qualities* for mastering **TRUE CALM.** By now you should be quite comfortable with the sequence of exercises that comprise the "dance" toward **TRUE CALM.** Remember to practice using these new skills together in the following sequence:

- Deep "Sigh" Breathing combined with Small Stomach "Sigh" Breaths. Continue breathing from your stomach as you...

- Relax your face and body muscles, with either method. Continue breathing and stay relaxed as you...

- Focus your senses externally - seeing, hearing and feeling in the moment. Keeping those senses awake and continuing to breath, stay relaxed....

- Visualize and feel your Little Sun, as it enters and warms your body, as it beams *Life Energy* throughout your body.

Wonderful! Get ready - we're going to add some premium, high-quality fuel for a <u>great</u> ride. When you open up your energy faucet, you will have a marvelous treat. You will be able to **feel** its delicious, joyous, soothing, invigorating, and emotionally ***Uplifting Energy.*** It feels great because this higher rate of vibration **is** the energy of joy. It **is** the energy of love. You won't really know how good it is until you taste it, and we taste our *Life Energy* by **feeling** it.

"He who tastes, knows. He who doesn't taste, won't leave anyone alone". Proverb

Dermis Probe by Idries Shah

At the energy level, we are also accomplishing something of even greater magnitude. We are...

LOVING OUR SELF

KEY GOAL

Fig. 7.3

CHAPTER EIGHT

ENERGY-LOVING YOUR SELF

"When the oven is hot, bake bread." Proverb[1]

With talented guidance, psychotherapy can promote growth and self-understanding in emotional and psycho-physiological ways. At the core of psychotherapy is the quest to know ourselves. Ultimately, the final goal is to be able to use this self-knowledge to truly love ourselves.

Usually this SELF-love is withheld and denied because we don't think we deserve to be loved, and because we don't know <u>how</u> to love ourselves outside of letting ourselves enjoy a naughty dessert without too much guilt. Many of us believe we cannot love ourselves <u>until</u> we achieve something: success, wealth, nice clothes, a beautiful, thin body, someone who loves us, or a good job. Too often we are dependent on other people to give us love because we are incapable of giving it to ourselves. Of course, this dependency often has a price, for it may come with having to do things and be in situations that we may not like - which may even be abusive - just to get that bone of love thrown to us on occasion. While getting out of abusive situations is at least within our control, we are still left wanting to feel love.

Fortunately there <u>is</u> a way we can give ourselves love. By opening up the flow of *Life Energy* in our chest or heart area, we are performing the act of loving ourselves at its most powerful and effective level: energetically. What does it mean to love ourselves?

At the energy level, SELF-love is a FEELING.

SELF-love is a joyous, rejuvenating sensation, because it is the act of directly feeling our *Life Energy*. However we think of it psychologically, loving our SELF energetically simply feels good! Increasingly as we practice, energizing our Little Sun boosts our moods and quickly uplifts our emotions and spirits. It recharges us emotionally, psychologically and physically. With our Little Sun beaming its *Life Energy*, we feel good inside, and we feel good about being ourselves. Actually, what we feel IS the energy level of our SELF. It is the being which we are.

SELF-love allows us to be on our own side more firmly, so that criticizing and berating ourselves becomes irrelevant, an outdated behavior at all levels. By energizing our Little Sun, we start to grow into being our own best friend, our strongest supporter. In turn, we then may become more generous with others, helping and encouraging them to accomplish their goals and improve their own lives.

By energizing our Little Sun, we gradually stop identifying ourselves with our "ego," which is the often critical, demeaning and berating small self, the product of years of conditioning, beliefs and low self-esteem we absorbed from the actions of our parents, teachers and societal institutions. We begin to shift inside, identifying ourselves more and more fully with our CENTER, our true SELF. Gradually our inner dialogue and internal perceptions become more benevolent and openhearted. We make a monumental shift in our relationship with ourselves, and others. With the support and love we gain from our Little Sun...

WE GROW UP.

Working at the energy level, we can achieve enormous growth that would otherwise require years of successful psychotherapy to accomplish, if ever. The mystery of this emotional, spiritual and psychic expansion can be explained at an energy level of understanding. By freeing our energy flows to circulate more fully within us, we gradually (or often quickly) dissolve the "stuck" energy patterns that show up as emotional problems, low self-esteem, insecurity and pessimism. This happens, in part, because our emotional problems, negative attitudes and even our physical conditions are held in place - *at the energy level* - by certain patterns, usually in the form of blockages in energy flow.

These unhealthy blockages can be dissolved with the accelerated flowing of the Little Sun's energy and replaced with increasing energy circulation. We accomplish this by energizing our Little Sun. Working at the energy level lets us grow inside - very directly. It's as if we are, sometimes at the speed of light...

***

ENERGIZING OUR SELF-ESTEEM

As we energize our Little Sun, our SELF-esteem rises. The extra energy flow makes us more positive, more optimistic, more up. We naturally focus more on our goals, the joys of our relationships, and the pleasures of life. We stop the process of powerfully energizing our problems, fears, anxieties and doubts by focusing on them so much. Those negative factors don't just disappear, but they no longer seem so large or so insurmountable. They don't require our constant attention. Problems become challenges to overcome.

In fact, with enhanced *Life Energy*, we have the clarity and perspective to see our fears and anxieties as necessary to help us to achieve our life goals and desires. Our resentment at even having difficulties can dissolve as we shift our thinking to regard our difficulties as useful, even benevolent partners in our growth. This more mature attitude allows us to understand that difficulties can lead us to decisions and actions that take us out of our comfort zones, allowing us to explore newer, grander areas of life.

SELF-esteem inevitably leads us to increasingly value this feeling of inner joy so that we naturally want to cultivate, expand and enjoy it. All we have to do is picture and energize our Little Sun with love and joy. The rest follows, often quite unexpectedly, and very pleasantly.

Little by little we become more aware of ways to enjoy ourselves, our lives and the people in our lives. Although energy measuring devices are developed which can verify and confirm electromagnetic changes, medical science is still focused on managing illness and has not yet recognized how subtle changes in energy flow can actually produce greater health. However, we don't need to wait. We can go ahead and **feel** more energy today, by practicing the steps for energizing our Little Sun. Keep in mind that by mechanically increasing your *Life Energy* flow, you are nourishing, respecting and loving your SELF at the energy level. Here's how to...

***

ENERGIZE YOUR LITTLE SUN

There is more than one way to energize your Little Sun. They all begin with the basic exercises you now know quite well - breathing, muscle relaxation and external auditory focusing, combined with visualization of your Little Sun. After your Little Sun is comfortably resting in the center of your chest area, beaming its light and filling you up with its *Life Energy*, you can stimulate it even more if you...

- Picture a light switch with a dial which brightens your Little Sun the more you turn it in the counter-clockwise direction. Move the dial as slowly or as quickly as feels comfortable. There is no "stop" point on the dial, so you can make the light as bright as you are able to visualize and feel it.

Or...

- Simply send good thoughts and feelings to your Little Sun. This helps open your inner faucet of *Life Energy*.

The best way, and the recommended way, to greatly strengthen your life force is to do the following:

***

HOW TO LOVE YOUR SELF
AT THE ENERGY LEVEL.

Step 1. **Perform the exercises you have mastered so far**, up to and including visualizing your Little Sun and drawing it into your body. Let your Little Sun settle peacefully in your chest and keep it radiant.

PREFERRED FOCUSING SENSE

internal

Step 2. **Generate within yourself feelings of love and joy.** You can produce these feelings by thinking about something or someone you love, on whatever really brings you joy. Your focus might be a person, a pet, a piece of art or music, a place, a flower, your favorite sweet dessert, a breath of fresh air, some activity that makes you feel really good - anything. Then... while you continue holding on to the actual feelings of love and joy, let go of the content of whatever brings you those feelings.

Step 3. **Send these feelings of love and joy right into your Little Sun.** The Little Sun responds very positively to these emotions and becomes energized from them. By focusing on feeling joy and love directly, you can feel your Little Sun enthusiastically receiving their gifts!

Step 4. **Open up inside more and more simply by letting go.** As you send these feelings of love and joy to your Little Sun, let the Little Sun radiate its light even more fully and freely.

Step 5. **Continue feeling (and feeding) your Little Sun** for as long as feels comfortable. Remember to keep yourself let-go, and hang out with this energizing process for 5 to 6 minutes as you are learning it. Great results come from focused effort.

Energizing your Little Sun becomes a two-way process. You are directing feelings of love and joy into your Little Sun while you are helping it grow and expand its own intensity within you, through consciously opening up the Little Sun - by <u>letting go</u>. In terms of your *attention-focusing*, you are now connecting several things together: the feeling of letting go inside with - the image of the bright, shiny Little Sun radiating its light throughout your body, the feeling of the center of your chest area, and the emotions of joy and love. (See Figure 8.1)

This opens up your faucet of *Life Energy*.

As you open up that faucet - through letting go more and more - you receive more **Life Energy**. And... you give this **Life Energy** to yourself!

Practice energizing your Little Sun daily for 5 to 6 minutes to gain optimal benefits. You <u>can</u> usefully spend longer amounts of time exploring and energizing your Little Sun. You can also quickly energize your Little Sun, even for a few seconds at a time, whenever you wish to feel more energy, to uplift your mood, and to feel good inside. Do this by picturing it in your chest area - bright and shiny - and feeling it radiating sensations of joy and love there.

A corporate attorney once related to me that she was walking down a hallway to a business meeting late one afternoon, feeling quite fatigued. While she was walking, she stimulated her Little Sun. She said that by the time she reached the meeting room door she was energized, refreshed and mentally alert - raring to go! She made the Little Sun practical in her life.

ENERGY-LOVING YOURSELF

Producing life energy with the Little Sun   *The feelings of love and joy open up the faucet of our Life Energy flow*

Fig. 8.1

      Be assured... if you let it flow naturally and trust it, you will only receive as much as is good for you, never too much. This is, after all, ***Life Energy***. It's for you to learn to use and enjoy, and you are not taking it away from anyone else. With only a little practice, you will quickly begin to appreciate...

***

THE BENEFITS OF ENERGIZING YOUR LITTLE SUN

When you energize your Little Sun, you mechanically create an amazing variety of wonderful and healthy events. It's like one-stop shopping for your mind, body, emotions and SELF-esteem.

First, you are mechanically and naturally generating greater energy - energy that is very different from the rough, jagged, frenetic energy of caffeine and sugar. This *Life Energy* does not use your adrenal glands, which may already be dangerously overtaxed from the constant stresses of daily life. Instead, the Little Sun generates pure *Life Energy* that is healing and rejuvenating. It's like pouring high-octane fuel into your "tank," with no biological or ecological downside. Correctly energizing your Little Sun will give you the unusual feeling of having energy <u>inside you</u> that is both invigorating and soothing at the same time.

Second, you are directly stimulating your thymus gland, which is a main gland for immune strength. So by energizing your Little Sun, you are directly strengthening your immune system.[2]

As a third benefit, you are mechanically improving your ability to accomplish your life goals. Volumes of books have been written testifying to the power of positive visualization. Olympic athletes, dancers, musicians, performers and public speakers are keenly aware of the advantages of mentally picturing themselves performing successfully. It's widely accepted and well-documented that by visualizing our goals we can speed up the process of accomplishing what we want. Practicing the Little Sun strengthens your ability to focus, to concentrate, to visualize and energize anything <u>else</u> you wish to improve.

In fact, you can now go beyond simply visualizing your goal. You can...

***

ENERGIZE YOUR GOALS!

Step 1. Picture a goal you want to achieve, and picture it clearly.

Step 2. Beam the image of your goal with the Little Sun's rays,

or...

Step 3. Bathe the image of your goal with your *Life Energy* by picturing it <u>inside</u> the Little Sun.

PREFERRED FOCUSING SENSE

internal

This greatly accelerates the <u>process</u> you may need to go through to achieve your goals. (See Figure 8.2) So put on your seat belt! This is how you...

***

ENERGIZE YOUR HEART'S DESIRE!

A beautiful friend of mine, a jazz singer, was berating herself because her career seemed to be disintegrating. Musicians weren't calling her to sing with them, and the gigs she did get somehow never worked out very well - they were often cancelled, one after the other, for various reasons. Finally, she went to a concert one night and saw people there she had worked with over the years - many of them she knew very well. But they didn't seem to recognize her, even when they looked into her eyes from ten feet away. She went home feeling depressed, invisible and somewhat worthless. As a last resort she spent a few days **energizing her Little Sun**, bathing in the feelings of love and joy that the Little Sun produces.

This was all she needed. Afterward she felt great, charged with the confidence in her SELF, feeling the direct connection with her SELF at the energy level that allowed her to relax inside and know that she could gracefully handle anything that might happen. Things in her life began to turn around. She received a call from some producers who were considering hiring her to write and perform theme songs for their television shows. If that same call had come a week earlier, her lack of confidence, i.e., her lack of *Life Energy*, would have probably turned the producers off. As it worked out, they loved her vibrancy and her calm enthusiasm, which gave them the confidence they needed to give her the job.

She was able to energize her Little Sun to boost her *Life Energy* because she understood two basic facts. First, she recognized that the string of unsatisfying events in her life was communicating a message she needed to receive. It was telling her that she needed to get in touch with her SELF by getting calm, going inside, and picking up the phone to find out what had changed.

Secondly, she realized she needed to nourish and recharge herself at the energy level - through the simple mechanical act of focusing on and energizing her Little Sun. She knew she needed to **love her SELF at the energy level.**

ENERGIZE YOUR GOALS

A major step toward accomplishing our goals is to identify each goal we want MORE OF. Visualizing our goals increases our ability to achieve them. Energizing our goals by picturing them bathing in our Little Sun's light further accelerates the process of goal achievement.

Fig. 8.2

In each and every situation, we can raise our moods, lift our spirits, and cleanse our emotions simply by generating a greater flow of *Life Energy*, connecting with our CENTER and becoming more "in the flow." We become changed, and suddenly external difficulties are more manageable, easier to handle. Rejuvenated, we have the strength to go on. (See Figure 8.3)

Perhaps most importantly, being able to generate powerful, bright energy with your Little Sun is...

***

THE SINGLE MOST IMPORTANT ANTIDOTE TO STRESS

Adaptation Energy

After a lifetime career of studying stress and its effects on biological organisms, Dr. Hans Selye, the grandfather of medical stress research, concluded that humans have a <u>basic energy supply</u>, which he called our "adaptation energy." Dr. Selye creatively researched and documented how the diseases of stress take increasing tolls on our energy supply, becoming more dangerous and life-threatening as our adaptation energy supply dwindles. Selye's definition of stress was "the non-specific response of the body to any demand."[3]

Dr. Selye charted three stages which describe the biological process of extinction through constant, unresolved stress reactions, which he called the "General Adaptation Syndrome." The first stage in this process is "Alarm," when the fight/flight emergency response is triggered for survival. We have discussed this thoroughly in previous chapters.

PREMIUM FUEL

Incredible, imagine that
Just two emotions serve to tap
Our wondrous source: *Life Energy*
Love and Joy achieve this deed.

They resonate to form the key
That opens wide this faucet free
Energetically, we'll see
What humans can become and be.

Scientifically it will be shown
We humans are much more than's known
Meanwhile we can feel quite fine
And come to grow what is divine.

Fig. 8.3

The second stage Selye described is "Resistance," when the body adapts to being in a survival mode, and our internal organ activity seems to become normalized again. Of course, this type of adaptation uses up large amounts of energy <u>when resistance to stress continues without relief</u>. Basically, we can now recognize this as resistance to change, and an attempted adaptation to living with a continuous, ongoing survival reaction. It's like pushing aside our upset emotions, headaches and tense neck muscles, so we can focus fully on accomplishing our goals at work. We succeed. And... we pay the price, for it takes energy to push these discomforts aside.

The third stage in the "General Adaptation Syndrome" is called "Exhaustion." This describes a kind of premature aging, due to the unrelieved and unrelenting wear and tear of unresolved stress. Immune systems weaken, illnesses develop, major organs deteriorate, and faster death results.

Dr. Selye beautifully described the process of unsuccessful adaptation to change. Since much of his research was performed on captive laboratory animals whose options were unnaturally restricted to "grin and bear it," his research findings were limited to the stress of unsuccessful responses. The animals were faced with change, but only in an experimental setting which held all variables constant except one. <u>The animals were effectively denied the possibility of creative or different responses</u>. However, thanks to his work, we now know very well what happens when we do not or cannot respond effectively to change. The same scenario results when we, like the animals trapped in laboratory cages, do not recognize and do not (or cannot) respond appropriately to our signals of *Change Awareness*. We die early or our species becomes extinct more rapidly.

Major organ deterioration, immune disorders, cancers, diabetes and illnesses leading to total exhaustion - ie. death - are directly related to the stresses of life taking their draining tolls on our adaptation energy supply. Owing to Selye's theories and research, life's changes, whether good or bad, have been associated with increased illness, because his belief was that adapting to any change is stressful, and uses up one's adaptation energy.

As we discussed in Chapter Five, change is in itself neither good nor bad. More depends on how we respond to change. Given what we now know, perhaps it would be more useful to describe stress as "the result of ineffective, unhealthy reactions to change." Then the door is opened for exploring "effective, healthy and positive responses to change," which results in human *THRIVING.* This is what growth is all about.

Throughout most of his fifty-year career, Selye considered this adaptation energy supply to be finite, an assumption that might make anyone fear change. But in his last book, *The Stress of Life*, which summarized his many years of work, Selye speculated in the final chapter entitled: "The Road Ahead," that *it was entirely possible that human adaptation energy could be increased*.[4] Using his words:

> Adaptation energy seems to be something of which everybody has a given amount at birth, an inherited capital to which we cannot add, but which we can use, more or less thriftily, in fighting the stress of life. Still, we have not fully excluded the possibility that *adaptation energy could be regenerated to some extent* [emphasis added], and perhaps even transmitted from one living being to another, somewhat like a serum. If its amount

is unchangeable, we may learn more about how to conserve it. If it can be transmitted, we may explore means of extracting the carrier of this vital energy - for instance, from the tissues of young animals - and transmitting it to the old and aging.[5]

Dr. Selye, of course, assumed that this increase in energy would come externally, from a new pill or medication. He stated that if humans could indeed increase their adaptation energy supply, then **this should be the primary focus of medical research**. Given the vast array of health problems and serious illnesses caused by limited *Life Energy* supplies, it would be central to improving the quality and quantity of life. Fascinating research will result when we turn loose scientists who also have the experience to know that this realm of energy exists. Greater levels of health will be discovered.

The Little Sun offers practical means to increase this adaptation energy supply. Thus it may well prove to be the most effective and most powerful antidote for stress - a direct boost to our immune strength. Energizing your Little Sun is a direct way to protect your health and enhance your overall well-being.

THE SUPPLY OF *LIFE ENERGY* IS FULLY ABUNDANT!

Many people over the years have gained experience with their Little Sun. At the first sign of difficulty, they have trained themselves to immediately focus inside and energize their Little Sun. Why not make your problems flow more smoothly as well? Sometimes we can dissolve difficulties simply by going inside and connecting up with our CENTER via the Little Sun. It's as if all that is required of us by our CENTER to smooth the difficulty is to open the energy flow to our true SELF.

While we don't often talk about it, we also know we feel other people's energy and are greatly influenced by it. When someone with big energy enters a room, he or she gets noticed, stands out, and has a presence. Talking with that person, we come away feeling stimulated, uplifted, charged up and feeling good.

On the other hand, being near a person whose energy level is very low also affects us, often leaving us emotionally and physically drained. They absorb some of our *Life Energy*. This can happen even over the telephone. Sometimes events and stressful situations take our energy, and we feel weakened afterwards, occasionally even falling ill. You can defend against problematic people and draining situations by "visiting" your Little Sun and replenishing yourself as soon as you need more *Life Energy*.

Keep in mind that your Little Sun is there to connect you with your SELF. It is there to protect and nourish you, because...

***

YOUR LITTLE SUN IS YOUR BIRTHRIGHT.

Your Little Sun is your *Life Energy*. It's your CENTER. It's the real you! Make your relationship with your Little Sun a delightful game. Be gentle and kind to yourself for making the effort, whether or not you are having success in "playing" with it. Some days, generating lots of energy seems to elude us, no matter how much we try. Other days it's just bursting within us to give us energy. At these times we might not recognize that our efforts of days and weeks past have accumulated to open up our inner faucet of *Life Energy*, just when we thought it was hopeless. So, keep trying. Your efforts WILL bear fruit. (Figure 8.4)

***

Your mastery of the basics of **TRUE CALM** is nearly complete. There is one remaining lesson - mechanical, of course! - that will lead you into new realms of personal growth, satisfaction, and joyous experience. The core idea is simple, the exercises are fun, and results are guaranteed. Fasten your seat belts, we're moving into high gear. We're going to use our *Four Treasured Qualities* to uplift ourselves out of the physical, mental, emotional and behavioral manifestations of our ancient survival response. We're moving up, into...

human *THRIVING*

KEY GOAL

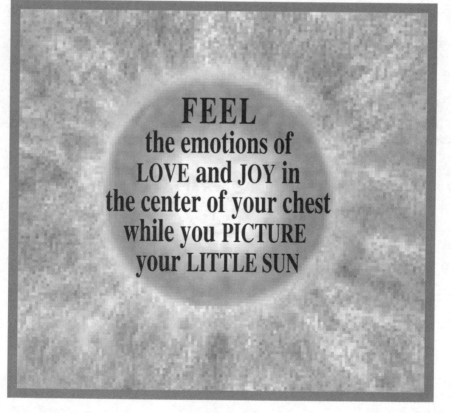

FEEL
the emotions of
LOVE and JOY in
the center of your chest
while you PICTURE
your LITTLE SUN

Fig. 8.4

THRIVING

"A man's capacity is the same as his breadth of vision."   Proverb[1]

At nearly every level of our functioning - behaviors, thoughts, emotions, and neurological organization - we have only two modes of motivation. How we operate at any time is largely determined by which of these instincts we are obeying. The "big picture" of our evolution shows, with the benefit of some hindsight, that humans have for many millennia been overwhelmingly dominated by only one of these motivations:

SURVIVING

The physiological activities, emotions, thoughts and behaviors driven by the survival instinct share a common theme. They are all designed to help us reduce, eliminate and get away from things which threaten us, things we don't want, or things we...

WANT LESS OF

Activities of defense, avoidance, cover-up, leaving, denial, containment, prohibition, exclusion, prejudice, banning, fighting, hatred, separation, detachment and confinement are the routine behaviors of surviving.

Fortunately, we are endowed with an additional motivation that is essential to survival itself. It propels us into another direction, toward connecting with, expanding into, and going toward things that appeal to us, things we do value and desire, things we...

WANT MORE OF

Growth, development, goal achievement, evolution, creativity, advancement, cooperation, inventiveness, progress, accomplishment, peacefulness, attachment, joy, happiness, confidence, sharing, love, friendship, inclusion, open-mindedness and success are all products of this impulse. They are connected to the fundamental life activity of *THRIVING*.

To illustrate the difference between these two ways of thinking and being, let's back up and consider an all-too-familiar frame of mind. It's called...

***

THE WORST CASE SCENARIO

Try this:

- Think of a stressful situation you are now experiencing in your life, or that is coming up for you. When you have focused on one situation and are ready to concentrate...

- For the next 2 minutes, close your eyes and imagine <u>all</u> the things that could go wrong in that situation.

And as those things go wrong, what <u>other</u> problems and difficulties could occur? How <u>bad</u> could it get? Remember, do this for <u>a full 2 minutes</u>. Then...

- **Notice how you feel**. Are there any changes in your breathing? In your muscle tension and in your heart beat? How did that way of focusing affect your stomach? How does your chest feel? What emotions of stress did you experience?

Feeling a bit... jumpy, are you? Sorry about that.

If you sincerely involved yourself with that exercise, you've had a fresh reminder of how intimate the connections among your mind, your body, and your emotions are. They all operate together as a complete organism, just as our hand includes all our fingers together. The uncomfortable feelings you just experienced show how our bodies react when we focus our attention exclusively in the direction of **surviving**, that is, each time we think about anything we want **LESS OF**. In fact, survival focusing automatically triggers ancient physiological survival reactions at <u>all</u> levels of our brain operation. At the energy level, it's like creating an instant magnet or electromagnetic force field: we focus on what we want **LESS OF** and we automatically feel repelled, as if we get pushed away from it.

On a very practical level, this means each and every time we begin feeling stress, emotional upset, racing thoughts, anxiety and panic attacks, it is precisely BECAUSE we are focusing our attention on something we want LESS OF. There is no mystery at work here, only the mechanics of how our mind and body operate together. To experience the opposite of **LESS OF**, let's explore...

***

THE BEST CASE SCENARIO

- Picture <u>the same stressful situation</u> you concentrated on in the previous exercise. This time, however...

- Keep your eyes closed for the next 2 minutes and imagine <u>the most wonderful things</u> that could happen in that same situation. You can keep it within the realm of reality, or you can let loose and fantasize wildly, imagining the best, most amazing scenarios developing in the situation.

- Continue to enjoy that fantasy for a full 2 minutes. No matter how fantastic or seemingly "impossible" your creative thinking becomes, don't stop yourself with "yes-buts" or "what-ifs." Just have fun with your fantasy - be creative!

- Focus on what you want **MORE OF** in the situation. As a few wonderful things start to occur, imagine what other great things and joyous opportunities can result. How marvelous can it get!?! How much joy can you feel? Now...

- Notice any changes in your body. **How do you feel?** Did all the tension and discomforts of the previous exercise go away? Did that bring you joy? An inner warmth? More energy?

If you felt radiant and happy inside, try to locate exactly <u>where</u> you felt this *Uplifting Energy.* You may be fascinated to discover it usually comes from the center of your chest area - the home of your Little Sun.

Comparing the two experiences, which one left you feeling stronger, calmer, more confident, and more joyful? Given a choice, would you rather focus on what you want...

MORE OF!
or...
LESS OF?

At any moment, this is an important question to answer for yourself, especially because with *Presence of Mind,* you have the chance - at any moment - to focus on what you want **MORE OF**. It's <u>your</u> mind!

MORE OF is the motivational direction common to people who are happy, healthy, creative and successful. In fact, the main difference between these more positive people and stressed-out, negative, depressed folks is the direction of motivation in which they are focused throughout their daily activities. When we are feeling great, uplifted and positive, it is precisely BECAUSE we are focusing on things we want **MORE OF**, even if this occurs outside our conscious awareness. Focusing on **MORE OF** is a mental secret for greater joy, happiness and fulfillment.

When we focus on whatever we want **MORE OF**, our motivation is automatically directed to make us approach, get closer to, develop, and reach for what we really want. Again, it's like creating an instant magnet or an electromagnetic force field. When we focus on what we want **MORE OF**, we get pulled toward it. And... we pull it toward us. It's mutual.

As mental creatures we need a **MORE OF** focus to reach our goals. With this type of focus, our motivation generates itself, so we reach our goals more quickly and easily. In fact, once we achieve a **MORE OF** focus, we have accomplished the greatest single step toward reaching our goals.

The combination of *The Four Treasured Qualities* of TRUE CALM with a MORE OF focus allows us to stabilize ourselves - physically, mentally, emotionally and energetically - in the uplifting motivation of *THRIVING* - whenever we want.

What exactly is *THRIVING?* A useful way to understand *THRIVING* - and to understand our urgent need for moving ourselves out of **surviving** and into **THRIVING** - is to trace the development of our basic motivations through the four general stages of our human brain development. You may want to know...

***

HOW YOUR BRAIN GREW

Over the long course of human development our brain has been changing physically with very practical effects on our lives. Overall it seems that our brain was "built" in four different stages, with new parts gradually developing to help us achieve stability within our ever-changing physical environment. (See Figure 9.1) At each stage of growth, our brain's activity has been organized around both *THRIVING* and **surviving**.

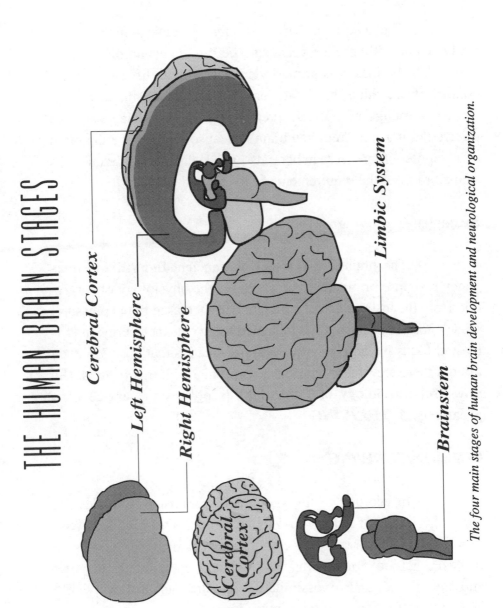

THE HUMAN BRAIN STAGES

Cerebral Cortex

Left Hemisphere

Right Hemisphere

Limbic System

Brainstem

Cerebral Cortex

The four main stages of human brain development and neurological organization.

Fig. 9.1

THE BRAINSTEM

The oldest part of the brain, the brainstem, probably evolved some 500 million years ago, before the evolution of mammals.[2] The brainstem is primarily concerned with life support: the control of breathing, heart rate, and basic metabolism, as well as danger warnings of possible predators or prey. Scientists have referred to it as the "reptilian brain" because it looks like the brain of a reptile. Many researchers also think this "basic brain" was shaped to meet the requirements of living in the ocean.[3]

Brainstem/Surviving

The brainstem is where the ancient **fight/flight** emergency response originated. As we know, the physiology of surviving, from the instant rush of adrenaline to increased blood pressure, muscle tension, and so on, is designed to give us the energy, mobility and focus we need to survive life-or-death situations. Yet even though there are times when sheer surviving is all that matters, **the powerful physiology of fight/flight is <u>always</u> in service of a greater goal: *THRIVING*.**

Brainstem/*THRIVING*

In addition to life support, the brainstem provides the basic physiology of *THRIVING* in the form of what is called **"feed and breed."** The brainstem's elaborate mechanisms for guiding us in desiring food; for hunting, recognizing, obtaining, cultivating and eating food; and for assimilating its nutrients have evolved to enable us to furnish our bodies with life-sustaining energy.

Our digestive system, for example, follows an ingenious

and elaborate procedure that begins with our seeing, smelling and even just thinking about food. Long before we taste the actual food, our salivary glands often start secreting their digestive juices and the muscular walls of our stomach contract. We experience this as "hunger pangs" that are guiding us to eat.

At each stage of the intricate process that follows, nutrients are sorted out and broken down into subtle, specific chemical combinations that distribute nourishment where it is needed. The unusable materials are handily discarded by elimination, guided by the wisdom of the brainstem. The nutrients we manufacture through digesting food sustain more than mere survival. They afford us the energy we need to move forward, to grow, to do and to be.

Equally complex mechanisms guide us in desiring sex, searching for and recognizing sexual mates, courting and attaining sex. These mechanisms have evolved to enable us to procreate and nurture children. The physiologies of "feed and breed" assure the continuation and evolution of our species. Successful reproduction - enough but not too much - is, of course, an absolute necessity for a species' survival.

At the physiological level of the brainstem, the motivation of **feed/breed** is very different from fight/flight's survival aim of getting rid of something we don't want, or moving away from a danger we want **LESS OF**. The *THRIVING* motivation is one of approaching, producing or embracing something we want **MORE OF**. (See Figure 9.2)

The survival impulse protects. The *THRIVING* impulse provides.

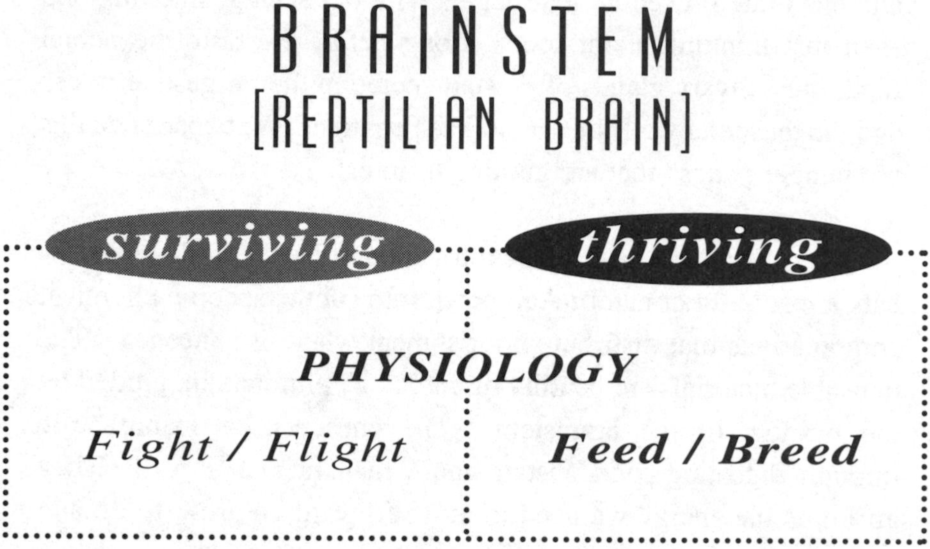

BRAINSTEM
[REPTILIAN BRAIN]

surviving ···· thriving

PHYSIOLOGY

Fight / Flight   *Feed / Breed*

Our two basic motivations expressed through the brainstem as primal physiological activities.

Fig. 9.2

THE LIMBIC SYSTEM

The second part of the human brain probably evolved some 200 or 300 million years ago.[4] Called the limbic system, it is often referred to as the "mammalian brain" because this same structure is found in mammals. Researchers believe the limbic system may have developed to meet newer needs of living on land, out of the oceans.[5]

The limbic system sits atop the brainstem and helps to maintain a stable environment within the body. Its "homeostatic" mechanisms regulate body temperature, blood pressure, heart rate and blood-sugar levels. Without the limbic system's stabilizing action we would be like the "cold blooded" reptiles, unable to adjust our internal climate to keep it stable when outside temperature conditions of heat and cold change. The limbic system also contains the hypothalamus, called "the brain of the body." The hypothalamus regulates eating, drinking, sleeping, waking, body temperature, hormone balances, heart rate, emotions and sex.[6]

With the development of the limbic system came the ability to experience emotions. More than simply physical creatures, we became emotional creatures as well. As we added on this new part of our brain, both the feed/breed and the fight/flight responses evolved their operations into the emotional realm.

Limbic System/Surviving

Adding emotions onto the physiology of surviving gives us the main emotions of fight and flight. At this level we experience the emotions we generally don't want, or wish to have LESS OF. The primary emotion of fight is **anger**. Diluting this primal emotion gives us its less intense variations: frustration, irritation, annoyance and aggravation.

The primary emotion of flight is **fear**. Diluted versions of fear are the emotional reactions of anxiety, panic, nervousness, worry, disappointment, concern, insecurity and even depression, as a flight inward from external reality. **All the emotions of stress are born from the fight/flight survival mechanism having evolved its operation into the limbic system.** Understanding ourselves in this way helps to take away both the mystery of stress and its powerful effects. The large variety of stress emotions share the same basic underlying structure.

Limbic System/*THRIVING*

The *THRIVING* motivation at the level of the mammalian brain also involves the emotions of feed and breed. The emotions of *THRIVING* are typically the ones we want **MORE** of. *THRIVING* emotions can feel quite delicious, especially in combination with the physiological roots of feed and breed. They feel much better than the stressful emotions of surviving for a reason: they are part of our natural, inborn guidance system for *THRIVING*.

Part of nature's grand design is for us to *THRIVE*.
This is why we feel so good when we are *THRIVING*.

The primary emotion of **feed** is **desire**. When we dilute desire we get less intense but very positive emotions like pleasure, fun, happiness, attraction, feeling turned on, wanting, enchantment and delight. (See Figure 9.3)

The primary emotion of **breed** is **love**. Physiologically, all desire is probably a form of love, using similar neurological pathways. The primary emotion of love is also associated with affection, caring, comfort, security, confidence (which comes from knowing, going for and having what you want **MORE OF**), joy, fondness, tenderness, liking, peace, hope, and feeling jolly.

THE CEREBRAL CORTEX

A rather recent stage of our brain development is the cerebral cortex, which came about some 50 million years ago.[7] The cerebral cortex is the executive branch of the brain; it makes decisions and judgments about all information coming into it, both from the body and from the outside world.

LIMBIC SYSTEM
[MAMMALIAN BRAIN]

surviving ⋯⋯ **thriving**

EMOTIONS

Fight / Flight ⋮ *Feed / Breed*

↓ ↓ ⋮ ↓ ↓

Anger *Fear* ⋮ *Desire* *Love*

↓ ↓ ⋮ ↓ ↓

Frustration	*Worry*	*Attraction*	*Affection*
Irritation	*Nervousness*	*Delight*	*Caring*
Annoyance	*Insecurity*	*Merriment*	*Tenderness*
Aggravation	*Anxiety*	*Happiness*	*Safety*
Resentment	*Panic*	*Fun*	*Confidence*
Bitterness	*Depression*	*Pleasure*	*Peace*
		Enchantment	*Joy*

Our two basic motivations expressed through the limbic system as our primal emotions and their derivatives of lesser intensity.

Fig. 9.3

As it organizes our inner and outer worlds, our cerebral cortex performs activities which enable us to adapt to change. It first receives information, and then analyzes it according to criteria which are mostly learned. It compares this new information with our stored information of prior experiences, wants, needs, and expectations. Then it makes decisions. Our health is largely regulated through these decisions and the resulting instructions sent by the cerebral cortex to our muscles, glands and organs.[8] Our whole body then responds in the ways necessary to achieve our goals of **THRIVING** and **surviving**.

Because our two directions of motivation operate in the cerebral cortex at a higher level of neurological organization, they can influence the activity of the two lower parts of our brain. This means our directions of motivation can affect our emotions and can override the immediate functioning of our physiological systems. **Practically, this means how we focus our attention either generates calm and the positive emotions of desire - love and joy - or stress and the upsetting emotions of anger and fear.** With our cerebral cortex regulating our bodies and activating the lower parts of the brain, the key for **THRIVING** is in learning to operate our own brain's...

***

EXECUTIVE ACTION

A major key for self-control, greater success, total health and happiness is choosing to direct our focus into the motivation of THRIVING.

Without exerting this control consistently enough to become automatic, we usually end up with our focus stuck in the motivation of **surviving**. We need to keep in mind that even though a compass has 360 degrees and we can walk in virtually any direction we want, when it comes to our motivation, we have only two directions to choose from:

CEREBRAL *THRIVING*

or

CEREBRAL SURVIVING

Have you ever wondered why, when your mind is racing anxiously, your thoughts aren't about happy, joyous, wonderful things? Somehow we end up focusing only on our worries, problems, anxieties, doubts and pains - all the things we don't want, all the things we want LESS OF. We may well ask "why?"

Through eons of conditioning, the mental patterns of surviving seem to get triggered automatically and quite easily whenever we encounter change. Whenever anything new, unexpected, different and unusual occurs, we tend to react with a survival response - even before we explore whether that change might be beneficial. For example, if we're walking through the woods and we suddenly hear a twig snap on the other side of some thick foliage, our first reaction is not, "Oh, good! That must be Bambi coming to visit with his family!" We immediately react with fight/flight. Mentally, we do the same. And that survival response is made more complex by our aptitude for...

LEAVING THE PRESENT, CEREBRALLY

At some point, probably when our brain evolved the cerebral cortex, we attained the ability to think abstractly, to conceptualize about things without their being physically present. For example, we can be working at the office when suddenly we start to think about how later that evening we'll be enjoying a delightful candlelight dinner with our favorite someone. Our imagination triggers feelings of pleasure as our taste buds become stimulated with the joys of the upcoming nourishment. Someone observing us can only conclude that our work really turns us on!

Of course, the ability to think abstractly can have the opposite effect. We can also be enjoying that candlelight dinner with our favorite someone when apprehensive thoughts of possible snags in the next day's business proceedings distract our attention. Our stomach gets nervous, our heart starts pounding, and we begin to perspire, losing our appetite for what's in front of us. Our sensitive companion might conclude that something is wrong with the meal, or worse, that we aren't interested in being there in the first place!

In both cases we were mentally able to leave the present moment. The first example made us feel great; the second probably did not. Both situations were produced and maintained <u>by how we focused our attention</u>. Even though directing this focus has traditionally been outside our control, we can now consciously make our minds work for us by consistently choosing to stabilize our...

FOCUS IN THE MOTIVATION OF THRIVING

It is most important to put our two motivations - surviving and *THRIVING* - into proper perspective to understand where we are going and to gain the benefits of both. Again, **at every level of operation, surviving is in the service of *THRIVING*. *THRIVING*** is the guiding light. Surviving serves to remove the blockages that prevent *THRIVING*, and surviving mobilizes our energy to overcome the challenges of accomplishing greater *THRIVING*. Within our quest for what we want **MORE OF**, we often must reduce, eliminate and overcome what's in the way of our growth.

Evolutionarily speaking, we are now very briefly poised at a grand and amazing juncture. It is grand because, for the first time in our recorded history, we are finally capable of moving beyond surviving to fully enter into our only other mode of functioning: *THRIVING*. Our present position is brief because we cannot in any case remain where we are.

It is magnificently ironic that the powerful motivation of surviving has taken us as far as we can go. Unless corrected, the very same thought patterns, emotions, physiology and behaviors of surviving that enabled us to endure this rugged physical-realm existence on planet Earth will be the source of our own extinction. The standard operating tools of surviving - fear, doubt, anger and uncertainty, with their resulting insecurities demanding greater and greater control - are simply no longer relevant for coping with the powerful forces of rapid global change. In fact, nearly all the effects that the survival motivation has on us have now become severe handicaps for navigating the future.

It is as if we've been racing forward with the momentum of millennia propelling us full speed ahead. The land around us is becoming increasingly devoid of wildlife and life-sustaining vegetation. In front of us we can see that the ground soon ends at the edge of an enormous cliff that drops off into a deep chasm - instant death. Then suddenly...

We see at the cliff's edge a solitary tree with a strong vine hanging from its branches. The ground we're running on is "surviving," with all its mental patterns, behaviors and emotions of dangerously adrenalized physiology. The tree is the body/mind state of **TRUE CALM**. The vine is our tool, our vehicle for crossing over to the other side, by choosing to focus our attention in the life-giving patterns of *THRIVING*.

We can use our speed, our momentum, and the vine to swing over the dangerous precipice and land safely on the other side, where we see beautiful forests, green grasses, clear lakes, sparkling rivers and lush mountains. All we need to do is grab the vine, swing and... let go at the right time.

Letting go of the vine at the right time requires *Presence of Mind*, being fully aware of what is going on in the present moment AS it is happening. Letting go means the ability to stop the "thinking" action of our brain enough to "perceive" what IS going on in the present. Letting go of the dominance of "thinking" as our main way of "knowing," letting go of our expectations, our predetermined needs, wants, prejudices and priorities, is crucial for seeing where we must go to ride the winds of change more calmly. We have successfully "thought" our way to the cliff's edge. To proceed, we need to now use other aspects of our perception: our intuition, our creativity and our abilities to see "the big picture." While letting go may be somewhat scary, continuing to hold on to the vine will only land us back in the barren landscape of surviving, without the momentum we need to cross again. This means extinction.

We need to use the tree's vine to cross over into *THRIVING*, over and over, every single time we encounter change. As described earlier, so-called "stress" is simply the result of ineffective, unhealthy reactions to change. The state of **TRUE CALM** in combination with the focus of *THRIVING* corrects that impasse.

***

WHY THRIVING IS ESSENTIAL

At the practical level of producing greater physical health, focusing our attention on what we want **MORE OF** increases our energy, well-being and happiness by stimulating the rich variety of brain and body chemicals that enhance pleasure and decrease pain. Brain research reveals that our thoughts directly produce physical substances in our brains, in the form of neuropeptides and neurotransmitters.[9] These tiny amino acids conduct nerve impulses throughout our brain and central nervous system. These same neuropeptides and neurotransmitters are found throughout our immune systems. Hence, **we are literally affecting our immune systems by our thoughts!** We are either boosting our immune strength by focusing on what we want **MORE OF**, or we are weakening our immune strength by focusing on what we want LESS OF. The feeling of radiating inside with joy and love, which you may have felt while doing the earlier exercise, is an experience of boosting your immune system through *THRIVING*.

Research and anecdotal evidence on people overcoming cancers, AIDS and other terminal illnesses show that the key ingredient for success involved the patients changing their self-images and expanding their lives into the things they want **MORE OF**. That is, they changed their internal mental activity from beating themselves up, criticizing and blaming themselves for their life situations, into mental activity which bathed them in affection, encouragement, love, forgiveness and respect. Such changes quickly result in a stronger will to live, because life begins to feel more worthwhile.

In changing your focus from surviving into **THRIV-ING**, it's helpful to understand something about unconscious results, or...

THE FINE PRINT

To gain the considerable benefits of **THRIVING**, we must **focus precisely and literally on what we want MORE OF.** The practical reason for such thoroughness is that our unconscious mind does not process words of negation. This means that the words "no," "none," "not," "less" and "never" are not recognized by our unconscious mind. For example, try this:

- Do NOT picture a pink giraffe with a green ribbon around its neck standing on a blue wheelbarrow. <u>Don't picture it</u>!

What happened? You probably saw the whole giraffe image inside your mind, colors and all, because the unconscious mind cannot make sense of the word "not." It's as if it doesn't exist. Our conscious mind can reject the picture, but only <u>after</u> it has appeared in our mind. Similarly, when we focus on things we don't want, on the things we want LESS OF, our body experiences them as stressful and automatically triggers fight/flight survival responses, including the emotions of fight/flight.

What happens if we say to ourselves or to others: "Don't think about that problem you have," or better yet, "Don't worry!"? We focus on the problem and worry anyway. Our body goes into some degree of fight/flight stress reaction, thus triggering survival activities at the other levels of brain activity. **Thus we cannot "NOT think" about something we want LESS OF. We must**

actively redirect our focus onto what we want **MORE OF.**
Doing so requires...

***

KNOWING WHAT YOU REALLY WANT

At a practical level of achieving our goals and desires,
we simply cannot produce what we want **MORE OF** by focusing
on what we want LESS OF. We can produce less of what we want
LESS OF, but that's it. Our two directions of motivation are not on
a continuum. If we get rid of what we want LESS OF, such as a
problem, we will not automatically have what we want **MORE OF**,
such as a goal.

For example, in the health professions we can now see
how the whole medical model is based on a surviving motivation.
Medical research and knowledge about humans has come from a
LESS OF focus on human pathology: disease, illness, problems and
dysfunction. Naturally, the motivation is to get rid of, reduce and
even try to eliminate the problems of poor health. Medical technology is at its best when confronted with acute problems of survival.

But even when the medical model achieves success and
completely eliminates a particular disease, we are merely and often
just temporarily "problem-free." We do not necessarily have the
robust, vibrant good health and energy we want **MORE OF.** We
simply do not have a health problem. We are in a state of neutral
health, not bad and not good. Most unfortunately, the entire sum
total of medical knowledge seems limited to interfering with, slowing down, reducing and eliminating problems of human health, a

LESS OF focus. Western medicine has not yet learned to produce positive health because it has focused exclusively on human illness.

With few notable exceptions, the field of psychology has also relied totally on learning about humans from human pathology, mental illness and emotional problems. Identifying, describing and producing a psychologically healthy, confident and flourishing person has not been accomplished. For example, this is why, strictly speaking, stress management and stress reduction can never achieve complete success, because the focus is still on stress - something we generally want LESS OF. Even if we were to rid ourselves of stress, what do we have? We might be momentarily stress-free, but we don't necessarily have what we want **MORE OF**, such as the *THRIVING* experiences of joy, calm, happiness, pleasure or confidence. We simply don't have stress.

Human *THRIVING* with positive physical, mental and emotional health can only be fully realized through a **MORE OF** focus. Research on what real health is and how to accomplish it should be our dominant focus, especially since producing true health nearly always prevents and overcomes the problems of poor health at the same time. We need a "Science of Optimal Health." The health care professions must now also evolve beyond the limitations of basic surviving, out of the traditional LESS OF focus. We advance and move into *THRIVING* by using...

***

THE BIG LEVER!

To move out of surviving into *THRIVING*, basically all we need do is switch our focus. (See Figure 9.4) We accomplish that by changing the content of our focus into what we want **MORE OF**. For example, instead of thinking "I want to manage my stress. I want less stress," we change our focus to "I want more calm, more confidence, more peace." This simple refocusing activates all the physiological, emotional, mental and energy-level patterns of *THRIVING*. Thus we begin the process of successfully bridging any gaps between where we are presently and the **MORE OF** we want to accomplish. The content will always be in the form of internal visual images and pictures, internal dialogue and sounds, internal kinesthetic sensations, perhaps some smells and tastes, all of which generate feelings. This next set of exercises shows you how. Use a pencil to write in this book or on a separate sheet of paper and take a few moments to thoughtfully fill in the blanks provided.

JOB *THRIVING*

- Name three things in your career or job that you want **LESS OF**. Then use *The Big Lever* to change them into three things you want **MORE OF**. For example, I want **LESS** time spent doing those parts of my work that I find boring, and **MORE** time spent doing those things that interest me. I want **LESS** worrying about my performance and **MORE** confidence that I'm doing my job well.

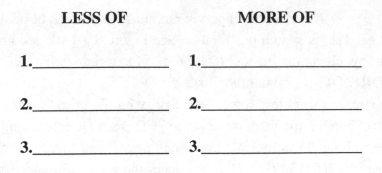

LESS OF   MORE OF

1._____ 1._____

2._____ 2._____

3._____ 3._____

RELATIONSHIP *THRIVING*

- Name three things in your relationship with some-one special or with several people in your life that you want **LESS OF**. Use *The Big Lever* to change them into three things you want **MORE OF**. For example, I want **LESS** arguing and **MORE** cooper-ation. I want **LESS** aloofness and **MORE** physical affection.

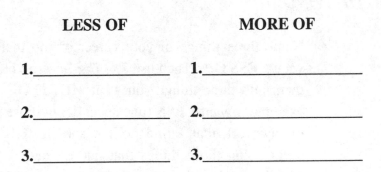

LESS OF   MORE OF

1._____ 1._____

2._____ 2._____

3._____ 3._____

SELF *THRIVING*

- Name three aspects of your relationship with your-self that you want **LESS OF**. Then use **The Big Lever** to change them into three things you want **MORE OF**. For example, I want to be **LESS** critical of myself and **MORE** supportive. I want to be **LESS** limiting of myself from changing and **MORE** encouraging of myself to get what I want **MORE OF** out of life.

LESS OF **MORE OF**

1._____ 1._____

2._____ 2._____

3._____ 3._____

Applying this simple concept in our lives installs new neurological patterns and gradually this becomes automatic. Fortunately, the **MORE OF** focus generalizes, such that the more aspects of our lives we apply it to, the more we benefit and *THRIVE.* It is evolutionary, since it lifts us out of the survival motivation that has dominated and greatly restricted our civilization's progress. It puts us into a new mode of operation that literally produces *THRIVING* with change, replacing the fear and anger responses of fight/flight which have been our automatic reaction to things new and different. The source of its simple power resides in the fundamental physiology of the brain, calling into play a beneficial set of...

***

MENTAL PATTERNS

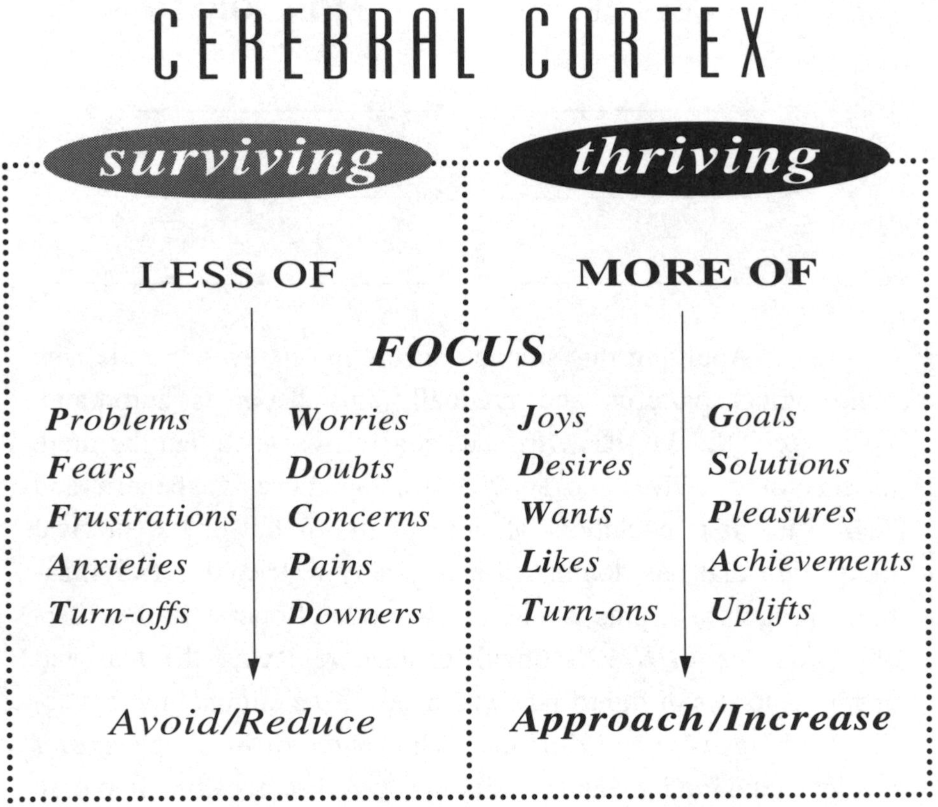

CEREBRAL CORTEX

surviving		*thriving*	
LESS OF		**MORE OF**	
FOCUS			
Problems	Worries	Joys	Goals
Fears	Doubts	Desires	Solutions
Frustrations	Concerns	Wants	Pleasures
Anxieties	Pains	Likes	Achievements
Turn-offs	Downers	Turn-ons	Uplifts
Avoid/Reduce		**Approach/Increase**	

Our two basic motivations expressed through the cerebral cortex as the two general directions in which we can focus our attention with their corresponding content and resulting actions.

Fig. 9.4

The Cerebrum

The fourth and most recent level of the brain to develop was the two differently functioning halves of our <u>cerebrum</u>, the huge mass of "gray matter" which comes to mind when we picture what our brain looks like. These two sides of our brain, referred to as the "right brain" and the "left brain," are physically separated by the corpus callosum, a bridge of some 300 million nerve fibers which connect these two hemispheres of our brain. This most recent area of brain organization probably evolved from 1 to 4 million years ago, and resulted in, among many things, the "left brain" controlling movement on the right side of our body, and the "right brain" controlling the left side of our body.

Functionally, the "right brain" is specialized for spatial functions like dancing, artistic expression, understanding how things are connected, recognizing how things fit together as part of larger patterns. The "left brain" function is specialized, in most people, for language and other sequential, step-by-step activities like thinking, analyzing and reducing things into smaller parts. (Separation into functions is only a general way of organizing our understanding, since people do vary and both sides of our brain are capable of performing both types of functions.) Generally speaking, the operation of this part of our brain results in certain different patterns of thought.

What is a Mental Pattern?

A mental pattern is a question we are in the process of answering within ourselves. For example, look around your physical environment right now and <u>count the number of things you can see that have the color blue</u>. Do this now before reading further.

You will notice that while you were looking for blue, you probably didn't notice all of the things with red or green colors. While concentrating on blue, you were excluding other colors from your focus. For another example, take a moment and identify the clothes you were wearing at 3:30 pm Sunday a week ago. Do this now before reading further.

You will probably find you recalled what you were wearing by remembering where you were, who you were with, and what you were doing, and that answering those questions began a process which filled your attention capacity. In other words, you probably were not thinking about eating, about reading a book, going to the store, what you will do tomorrow, being in the first grade, or a thousand other possible thoughts.

Using a mental pattern is like putting a colored filter, say a green one, on a camera lens. We only see green, no matter what we look at, because our conscious attention capacity is limited and easily filled with a single mental pattern. **Mental patterns serve to focus and concentrate our attention, but at the same time they limit our perception to the specific question we are answering by excluding everything else we could be thinking about and focusing on.** Keeping this dual characteristic of mental patterns in mind, let's examine the four main mental patterns of surviving, and of *THRIVING*.

Mental Patterns of Left Brain/Surviving

There are four primary thought patterns which function to lock our focus into the surviving motivation, based around determining what we want **LESS OF**.[10] These patterns are quite familiar; we jump to them whenever we have problems to solve or difficulties to resolve. These patterns are:

1. **What is the problem? (What makes this problematic?)**
2. **Why do I have this problem?**
3. **Whose fault is it? (Who is to blame?)**
4. **What other difficulties can this problem cause?**

To illustrate, try this:

Step 1. Pick a stressful situation, a problem or a difficulty you are currently experiencing.

Step 2. Analyze your problem or stress by answering the four mental patterns of surviving. Do not make an effort to solve your problem, simply answer the questions and explore where this leads.

Did you solve your stress by using those mental patterns only? If you followed the instructions strictly, then you probably organized your thoughts about your problem, but didn't come up with a solution. Why not?

While these mental patterns are commonly used to "problem-solve," they are not the patterns for solutions because **they keep us focused on what we want LESS OF: the problem**. Let's look at the assumptions behind them:

1. What is the problem? This pattern focuses our attention on analyzing, dissecting and describing the problem. It assumes that when we thoroughly understand all aspects of the problem, we will somehow know how to solve it. Of course this result is not guaranteed, and we can spend hours, days and months going over every piece of our problem forwards and backwards with no solution forthcoming. This pattern can use up much time and energy without producing the desired results of a solution.

2. Why do I have this problem? We seem to be addicted to answering the question "WHY?" in this culture, assuming that if we know "why," we will somehow know "HOW" to solve it. Actually, asking "why" takes us back in our minds on a historical journey into the past to reconstruct the series of events leading up to the problem. But because we missed the building up of the problem the first time through, any reconstruction we achieve will probably be sketchy and incomplete.

In the field of psychotherapy, asking "why" can be quite an involved, lengthy and expensive process. Even if we realize the "reason" why we have the problem - it was our mother, our brother, a mean teacher, the person who took away our rubber ducky when we were two years old, or what occurred three lifetimes ago - we still have the problem. Knowing "why" is no guarantee for knowing a solution.

3. Whose fault is it? While it is wonderful to have someone to blame, in actual fact whether we identify someone else or ourselves as the cause, this pattern still doesn't bring us any closer to a solution. Blaming someone else whose cooperation we need to accomplish a mutual goal only serves to create resistance from them, which adds an extra problem to resolve before we can proceed with solving our situation. This is the pattern of arguments. Unless someone actually messed up deliberately and spitefully, we can more usefully assume that we all, including ourselves, are doing the best we can and weren't trying to cause problems. This familiar pattern provides us no great service when we need solutions.

4. What other difficulties can this problem cause? This pattern effectively amplifies any problem, giving it the quality of "greatness." Focusing on generating more and more difficulties out of the current problem makes this the single mental pattern of hopelessness and helplessness. It seems to focus our limited attention capacity on remembering similar problems we have had in the past, and from this pessimistic and stressful state we then project into the future a view of life as a constant continuation of those problems. Keeping our focus on problems triggers the fight/flight response, so the imagined future feels, looks, sounds and seems perfectly gloomy. Disappointment and depression set in quite naturally.

These focusing patterns of surviving work in a very mechanical manner, locking our focus on what we want **LESS OF**. **It is virtually guaranteed that whenever we are feeling stressed, anxious, depressed and emotionally upset, it is BECAUSE we are focusing our attention in some combination of these four mental patterns.**

However, before we discard these patterns altogether, it should be noted that these patterns are quite fabulous at <u>organizing</u> our thinking about problems. A proper use is to take our problem and run it through these patterns of surviving. By doing so consciously and with clarity, we can save much time and anguish, while satisfying our curious analytic mind. Then we are free to go about finding the solution by using the four main mental patterns for solutions, which are the attention-focusing patterns of *THRIVING*.

Mental Patterns of Left Brain/*THRIVING*

Following are the four main mental patterns[11] that stabilize our focus on what we want **MORE OF**. They help keep us in the motivational direction of *THRIVING*.

1. **What do I want MORE OF?**
2. **How can I achieve it?**
3. **What resources do I have to begin now?**
4. **What opportunities might this goal generate?**

To illustrate how they work, try this:

Step 1.   Focus on the same stressful situation, problem or difficulty you chose in the previous exercise. Summarize or state it in terms of something you don't want, something you want **LESS OF**.

Step 2.   Use ***The Big Lever*** to change your focus in that situation into something you want **MORE OF.**

Step 3.   Now use the four mental patterns of ***THRIVING*** to explore that situation or problem by asking yourself the four basic questions noted above. Each of them involves using the focus of **MORE OF**.

Did you solve, resolve or at least discover a direction for solving your problem? How do you feel inside from using these mental patterns of ***THRIVING*** compared to how you felt from using the mental patterns of surviving?

Usually we feel much more optimistic and positive from keeping our focus on what we want **MORE OF**. Whether used consciously or naturally, these are the attention-focusing patterns which take us from a problem-oriented focus into discovering the creative solutions we seek. These are the mental patterns of solutions. There are practical reasons why.

1. What do you want MORE OF? Using this primary focusing pattern of *THRIVING* pinpoints our goals and begins to generate the details of how to accomplish, achieve and create what we want. The essential requirement is that our particular focus is indeed described as **MORE OF**, and not something we don't want.

2. How can I achieve it? This pattern focuses us on the game plan or strategy we need to best accomplish our goal, that which we want **MORE OF**. Without the goal, no amount of planning is effective. An old proverb says it this way: "For a ship with no destination, no wind is a fair wind." Given our limited conscious attention capacity, the sooner we can free our focus from the process of choosing our goal, the sooner we can focus on the next step: "how to." The freedom to work out the details for achieving a goal accelerates our attainment of what we want. This freedom comes only when the **MORE OF** goal is clearly in mind.

3. What resources do I have to begin now? This pattern focuses our attention on the business of starting, on taking the actions we need to "get the ball rolling." It allows us to perceive and to organize our perception in terms of producing our goal so the people, information, skills, material, knowledge and experience we have access to can become organized around producing our goal. It also serves to focus us in the present with our goal, so that we are already involved in accomplishing it.

4. What opportunities might this goal generate? This pattern focuses us into the quite-practical mental activity of future planning for the best case scenario. In other words, what happens if and when we actually do achieve our goal and we do get what we want **MORE OF**? We will want to "keep the ball rolling" through already knowing what else we want. By having mentally anticipated the eventuality of getting our goal, and by having focused beyond that goal to what we want to happen next, we have a greater chance of recognizing opportunities in the present and grabbing them as they occur.

As adults, we can keep firmly in our mind that **imagining a best case scenario does not mean we need to believe it will magically happen,** or that we must then expect it and be disappointed if things go differently. By planning for success we are not "setting ourselves up for failure." Instead, we are opening ourselves to a wider mental arena for accomplishment, satisfaction, and spontaneous discovery. (See Figure 9.5)

It is a simple and practical matter that the greater percentage of our time which is spent focusing on what we want **MORE OF**, the greater is our probability of actually realizing our goals. With our limited attention capacity, how would it be possible to achieve our goals, or even to know what our goals are, if we aren't focusing on them? The **MORE OF** focus leads us into a deep and elegant process that is extremely powerful when we **USE IT**.

A businessman was referred to me who had very high blood pressure (250/140) and who had been hypertensive for 10 years, despite a large array of medications. Every time doctors measured his blood pressure, they would rush him to a hospital, because normal, healthy pressure is 120/80. He was about to pop.

His doctor, whose specialty is reversing hypertension and helping people get people off medications, put him on a salt-free diet and instructed him to eat more nutritionally healthy meals and exercise regularly.[12] The results were frustrating. Recognizing mental stress as the culprit preventing his patient's healing, the doctor convinced the patient to see me. We discovered that he was raising up his blood pressure and keeping it elevated by keeping his focus constantly stuck in the mental patterns of LESS OF, the surviving focus. His internal organs were in a continuous fight/flight mode, with no relief. With the skills for calm, and learning to move his focus into **THRIVING**, his blood pressure immediately dropped 50 points in one week, and after 5 sessions was normalized at 140/90 and lower. Daily calm kept him healthy, and the **MORE OF** focus, applied vigorously in all areas of his life, made his relationships with his family, friends and his business a joy for all.

CEREBRUM
[LEFT HEMISPHERE]

surviving   thriving

MENTAL PATTERNS

Problems

What is the problem?*
Why do I have this problem?
Whose fault is it?
What else could go wrong?

Solutions

What do I what MORE OF?*
How can I achieve it?
What resources do I have to begin now?
What opportunities can this goal generate?

Our two basic motivations expressed through the cerebrum as mental patterns of left brain analysis.*Adapted from Neuro-Linguistic Programming® as developed by John Grinder and Richard Bandler.

Fig. 9.5

An additional, indeed, a primary benefit of the **MORE OF** focus is a more intimate connection to our intuition, our "Big Mind," our CENTER.

Mental Patterns of Right Brain/Surviving

The patterns of *THRIVING* mechanically operate to produce solutions, understanding and greater wisdom because they take us into the more right-brain opening of perception that a **MORE OF** focus naturally generates. Unfortunately, modern science and much of Western thought has overvalued the left-brain process of "analyzing" to such an extent that we seem to have learned only to reduce, dissect and separate into smaller and smaller parts. This particular way of focusing on smaller and smaller parts has mechanically had an overall limiting effect on our ability to perceive, particularly with respect to developing wisdom.

Called "reductionism," left-brain analysis too often operates like this: we focus on the general category of trees, and then we narrow the focus more and more specifically to certain types of trees, say fruit trees. We then reduce to apple trees in particular, then to a specific apple tree, then to one branch of that tree, to a single apple - and then we go inside that apple to its core and finally to a single seed within the apple's core. Perhaps we use electron microscopes to further isolate parts of a single cell within the seed. That's reducing to smaller and smaller parts.

The assumption of many scientists and thinkers seems to be that by finding the most basic elemental part, we will understand the "truth" of how things work. Somehow, it is assumed, identifying this basic smallest part will allow us to understand the "essence." Yet somehow, with each smaller part we discover, we still don't get the "big picture." We continue to imagine our lack of understanding exists because there's yet another smaller, more basic part to be discovered which will provide the missing piece of the puzzle, and off we go dissecting again. We seem to use this way of attention-focusing for almost everything, helping "reductionism" to become an almost automatic perceptual pattern. Developing that ability to analyze has powerfully evolved our left brain functioning tremendously, but that has unfortunately occurred at the cost of our right brain's fuller development, which is now needed for moving into *THRIVING*.

Mental Patterns of Right Brain/*THRIVING*

By focusing in the **MORE OF** direction of *THRIVING* and especially by imagining the best case scenario, we are performing an activity that directly connects us with the guidance and direction of our CENTER, the source of our creativity and intuition. The **MORE OF** focus mechanically functions to open our perception to the greater possibilities inherent in *THRIVING*, giving us our general direction in which to proceed. The wisdom of our CENTER operates very naturally through the **MORE OF** focus. Knowing where we want to go allows us to use everything that happens, everything we experience, and everything we learn as steps to accomplish our goals and desires.

It is no accident that the **MORE OF** focus of *THRIVING* naturally attracts us, while the LESS OF focus of surviving repels us. *THRIVING* is our guidance system operating to put us in an "approach" mode. Surviving is our guidance system operating to put us in an avoidance mode. **Both** are necessary. However, we cannot get where we want to go merely by backing away from the things we want to avoid in life. We must avoid life's potholes WHILE going towards the things we want **MORE OF**. (See Figure 9.6)

CEREBRUM
[RIGHT HEMISPHERE]

surviving   *thriving*

PERCEPTUAL PROCESSES

Reducing to Smaller Parts

Analyzing

Dissecting

Separating

Contrasting

Discriminating

Comprehending the Big Picture

Relating

Connecting

Matching

Agreeing

Recognizing Patterns

Our two basic motivations expressed through the cerebrum as perceptual meta-patterns of right brain cognition

Fig. 9.6

THRIVING WITH CHANGE

With practice we find we can become aware of and catch our CENTER's gifts of communication without needing to fully exclude our external focus in the world outside our head. We can cultivate becoming continuously tuned to our CENTER's guidance by being aware of our body-talk signals of **Change Awareness.** This is a more interesting, pleasurable and effective way of being in the world than to be "hit over the head" with the awareness of change in order to make us wake up.

Since, as a focal point, the Little Sun represents our core energy or our CENTER, daily energizing of the Little Sun literally opens up the channels of communication between our CENTER and our conscious mind. Energizing the Little Sun is an integral part of choosing the state of *THRIVING*. It continually increases our awareness of change and offers a direct, quick and practical path to evolving ourselves in the ways that many people on spiritual paths seek. The *THRIVING* focus speeds us in the task of...

***

GETTING WISER

While moving from a LESS OF focus to a **MORE OF** focus is a simple concept, actively putting the **MORE OF** focus in our daily lives is a new neurological event for human brain functioning. By producing more and more neurological connections, the **MORE OF** focus nurtures us at the physiological level by literally generating an increasing number of neurological pathways for our nerve impulses to travel along. This translates into more options, more creative solutions, new concepts and a growth of brain utilization.

In other words, by using the MORE OF focus, we become smarter. In the business world we can operate at the vanguard by conceiving and developing the new products, goods and services for a twenty-first century world of human *THRIVING*. We are expanding our perceptual capacities simply by focusing our attention in the **MORE OF** direction of *THRIVING*. **The MORE OF patterns of *THRIVING* naturally generate genius by moving our consciousness more and more fully into the greater awareness and expanded understanding of our CENTER.**

As we use the *THRIVING* focus and generate neurological connections exponentially, we eventually reach an expanded capacity to perceive. We mechanically grow a cherished quality of wisdom, the ability to perceive "the big picture." (See Figure 9.7)

The saying, "the whole is greater than the sum of its parts," is quite true, and so we need to be able to perceive a whole when one is operating. The practical truth of this statement also points to the deficiency of thought inherent in spending so much effort searching for the absolute smallest basic part as THE method for understanding the operation of something. It simply will not be understood that way. This is why "stress" cannot be successfully remedied without knowing its big picture: that it is how our *Change Awareness* signal guides us benevolently through change.

We don't need to discard the reductionist patterns of surviving's **LESS OF** focus. The tendency to think that either we use surviving's focus <u>or</u> we use the focus of *THRIVING* is another perception-narrowing offshoot of the left brain's limited attention capacity. This is the dreaded "EITHER... OR Syndrome," which operates every time we assume that reality is either one thing or another, white or black, right or wrong, light or dark, yes or no, good or bad.

Reality is more often composed of many options and levels, all existing simultaneously. "BOTH... AND" is a more useful and expansive thought pattern for *THRIVING*. We can keep the analytic thought patterns of surviving and ADD to them, so we have **MORE** options. Whether we as individuals consciously accept or resist this further evolution of our perception, our species will continue its accelerated leap into all that *THRIVING* is opening up for us. (See Figure 9.8)

OUR CALM GEAR

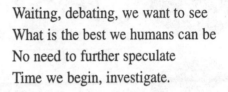

Waiting, debating, we want to see
What is the best we humans can be
No need to further speculate
Time we begin, investigate.

The way to get there is explore
All of which we do want MORE
Automatically this sets in place
A different kind of human race.

Our creativity's a plus
To bring out the greatness inside us
Actions, products, goods, ideas
Based on THRIVING, not on fears.

Our next evolutionary step involves using our innate calming mechanism to THRIVE with change.

"Heaven on Earth," "The Golden Age"
We've heard of these since ancient days
What if they're not mere fantasy
But future memory, our destiny.

Fig. 9.7

BRAIN EVOLUTION AND HUMAN MOTIVATION

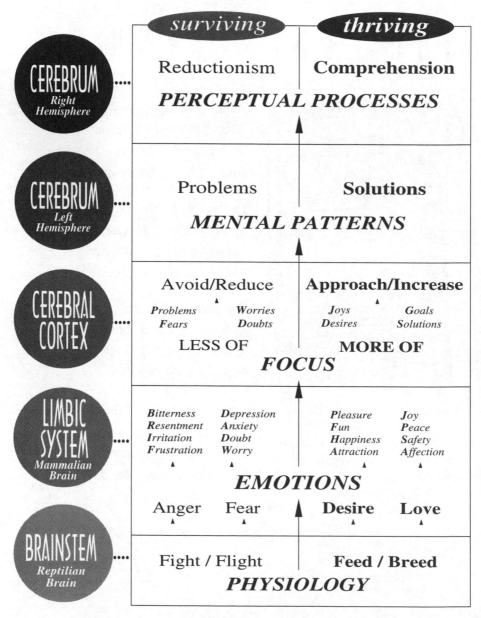

A general model for understanding how our basic motivations manifest through the four main stages of brain development and neurological organization.

Fig. 9.8

As the nations and peoples of our planet become increasingly inter-dependent, our ability to comprehend on a global scale is a major skill to incorporate into our mental activities. The **MORE OF** focus naturally increases our capabilities for thinking globally. After finally accomplishing "survival" and having the technology to eat, stay warm, and protect ourselves from the elements, we now get to move beyond surviving into *THRIVING*. It appears that we were "meant" to *THRIVE*. In fact, the hallmark of twenty-first century innovations will be that they are goods and services developed for human *THRIVING*. (Figure 9.9)

***

You have now received complete instruction in the steps toward **TRUE CALM**, and we have explored together some of the vast potential for using **TRUE CALM** as a tool toward *THRIVING* in your daily life. You are now ripe to master the practical six-second skill of...

instant calm!

KEY GOAL

CHANGE
your focus from
LESS OF to MORE OF
what you want in
every area of
your life

Fig. 9.8

CHAPTER TEN

INSTANT CALM

The Six-Second Skill

"Opportunity's precious, and time is a sword." [1]

*C*ongratulations! If you have practiced regularly, you are becoming proficient at the four basic skill areas of **TRUE CALM**. You are now ready to combine them to produce all *Four Treasured Qualities:*

Emotional Peace	*Physical Relaxation*
Presence of Mind	*Uplifting Energy*

within six seconds!

If you haven't yet honestly worked through and mastered the skills we have explored, you may want to take some time to do so. Reading about them isn't the same as actually <u>knowing</u> them. Without some experience in focusing your attention internally in the precise ways that produce the results you want, you simply will be settling for a second-hand, intellectual experience. **TRUE CALM**, and *instant calm* are achieved through mechanical exercises, but they are based in **feeling.** So if you still need to, take the time to go back and review any exercises you may have skipped over.

Remember that awaiting you is a wonderful sense of confidence that comes with knowing, especially during a so-called stressful situation, that you are simply responding to change in a healthy way, and that your intuition is benevolently guiding you to respond effectively and positively to whatever is changing. *Instant calm* will give you this special confidence and help you replace stress with a feeling of adventure.

The handy skill of *instant calm* quickly stops the stress reaction by turning off the sympathetic nervous system's arousal action, and by turning on the calming action of our parasympathetic nervous system. This gives you clearer access to your intuition through your position of greatest personal power, your home base in time: the present. You can then calmly embrace change and focus your attention as you choose, on what you want MORE OF, free of the fear-based and anger-based restrictions of surviving. What a liberating option to give yourself!

***

Instant calm is easily accomplished by combining your new understanding about attention-focusing with the individual focusing skills that we have learned. Basically, we integrate all of the previous skills into the three steps of a single Deep "Sigh" Breath.

HOW TO FEEL INSTANT CALM

Step 1. **Deep Inhale -** While inhaling deeply, energize yourself by picturing and **feeling** your Little Sun in the center of your chest area. As you inhale, feel your Little Sun becoming more and more energized, as if the air you're breathing is itself fuel for your Little Sun's fire. Focus on feeling the faucet of your *Life Energy* open up fully as you inhale.

PREFERRED FOCUSING SENSE

internal

Step 2. **Passive Release -** While exhaling in the "sigh for relief" fashion, use the momentum of the exhale to release the control levers of the nine major muscle groups involved in tension and stress. Release them like a wave of relaxation flowing from your forehead to your feet. Practice this by focusing on the passive muscle relaxation described in Chapter Three. Focus on feeling the

PREFERRED FOCUSING SENSE

internal

release "levers" for each muscle group as you are exhaling: forehead, eyebrows, eyelids, eyes, cheeks, jaws, shoulders, arms, hands, stomach, thighs, calves and feet. Then...

Step 3. **Rest -** Keeping your muscles in the "let-go" position, extend the rest period after exhaling and enjoy the respiratory "pause that refreshes" <u>before inhaling again</u>. At the same time, focus your attention in the auditory external mode, <u>listening fully and naming to yourself each and every sound going on around you in the present</u>. This is how you quickly establish *Presence of*

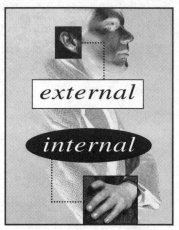

PREFERRED FOCUSING SENSE

external

internal

Mind, clearing your mind of distractions, worries and racing thoughts. It will immediately increase your awareness of and contact with reality.

***

HOW TO PRACTICE

Try these three steps, giving yourself only six seconds to feel calm. You may find that at first it's very easy to do some of these steps thoroughly, but others, for example certain muscles, are more difficult to relax so quickly. Simply do *instant calm* again, this time focusing more on whatever part seemed more difficult to accomplish.

It is important to give yourself only six seconds so that within this self-imposed time limit, you can become better and better at feeling **TRUE CALM**. You will greatly improve your efficiency with practice! Challenge yourself to master *instant calm,* <u>especially</u> in real life, pressure-cooking situations. (Figure 10.1)

INSTANT CALM

Effects of stress need cause no longer
Damaged health, frayed thoughts to ponder
A single skill will activate
A clearer way to feel and think.

One breath cycle is all we need
To gain calm's soothing, slower speed
Quickly free we get a grip
Refocus, change and then uplift.

Fig. 10.1

Practice also doing *instant calm* with your eyes open, focused on a single spot. Be in charge of your own attention-focusing. See how deeply relaxed, how mentally clear, how emotionally calm, and how energized you can feel in six seconds. And keep in mind...

Letting go is the key...

Throughout this book I have frequently used the phrase "letting go." The physical, mental and emotional problems of stress are about "holding on." When stressed, we literally hold on with our breathing. Under stress, we hold our muscles tight, tensing them in reaction to events long passed or not yet occurring. With our attention focusing, we hold on mentally to stress-producing fears, worries, doubts and anxieties we want LESS OF. At an energy level, we are holding back the flowing of our life force. Stress is about holding on.

TRUE CALM is about letting go. We let go with our breath by performing the Deep "Sigh" Breath" and the Small Stomach "Sigh" Breath, especially by spending more of our breath cycle resting after exhaling. With **TRUE CALM** we dissolve muscle tension by letting go of the release levers for muscle control, and allowing our muscles to <u>remain</u> let-go when they are not in use. Mentally, we let go of racing thoughts and worries by focusing our attention on hearing external sounds, as they are happening. This frees us from the fear-based and anger-based mental patterns of stress, and stops the stress-producing process of "thinking."

We enter the process of "perceiving." Energy-wise, **TRUE CALM** allows us to let go of restrictions on our energy flow and to open the faucet of our *Life Energy*. With **TRUE CALM**, we operate all four systems together by letting go. With *instant calm* - in a single breath cycle of inhaling, exhaling and resting - we can mechanically achieve those results within six seconds!

While you will find *instant calm* immensely valuable in your daily life, you by now probably know how much nourishment and pleasure you can gain from daily practice of the skills you have learned in this book. *Instant calm* is a practical tool for any stressful situation. Fully enjoying the state of **TRUE CALM** with your Little Sun shining for 5 to 6 minutes is <u>a daily health necessity</u>. This may be why you're hearing a strong message from your "sixth sense" inviting you to...

***

PLEASE CONTINUE!

Experience how your life changes for the better as you operate from greater calm, more *Presence of Mind*, and increased energy. Feel your effect on others in your life, at home and on the job. Continuing to explore the fullness of each element of **TRUE CALM** for a few minutes daily can bring truly amazing benefits into your life. Explore how **TRUE CALM** cultivates your direct communication with your own CENTER. Use **TRUE CALM** and *instant calm* to get in touch with this wondrous aspect of yourself, to go inside yourself for the answers, guidance and understanding you desire. (Figure 10.2)

Especially continue to use these skills to fully open up the flow of your *Life Energy* with your Little Sun. It will continue to open and bring you gifts of joy and increased *Life Energy* for years to come. The most valuable gift is that of SELF love. It is a healthy act of love to generate **TRUE CALM**. And it's a proven way to enjoy your SELF, and love your SELF!

A single skill remains for you to enjoy. Let's put all the **TRUE CALM** skills together in a practical way that will make it easier for you to...

THRIVE with life's changes.

KEY GOAL

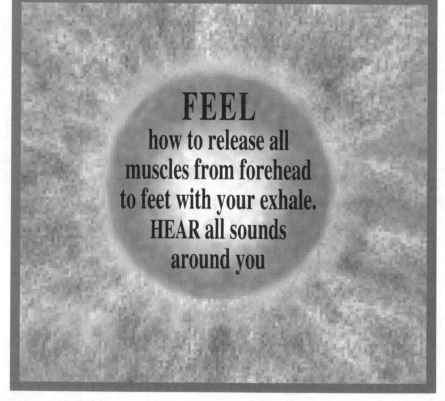

FEEL
how to release all
muscles from forehead
to feet with your exhale.
HEAR all sounds
around you

Fig. 10.2

CHAPTER ELEVEN

THE THRIVING RESPONSE

"Learning without action is like wax without honey."   Proverb[1]

How To Use TRUE CALM To Successfully THRIVE With Rapid Global Change And The Stresses Of Daily Living

*C*ongratulations! If you have practiced the preceding skills enough to make them work effectively for you, then you have accomplished something quite remarkable.

You are now in an unique and enviable position which very few of your fellow humans throughout history have ever been able to enjoy. You can now...

Change your own internal state.

Simply by focusing your attention, you can improve your state of "being" - of mind, body, emotions and energy. And you can do so quickly enough to forever stop being at the mercy of your ancient physiological survival mechanism, the fight/flight survival response. Breaking free of the stranglehold which survival has had on humans for millennia - by keeping us locked into its tyrannical effects at all levels of brain operation - is a considerable achievement in the course of human events.

With the **TRUE CALM** skills you can now dissolve, remedy and prevent the enormous damage which destructive stress causes on human health, happiness and decision-making. Even more importantly, you can now go beyond the physical, emotional and mental realms by further opening up the faucet of your own life force, enjoying more and more *Uplifting Energy*.

What all this means is, for perhaps the first time in our recorded history, as individuals and as a species, we can now...

Choose to respond positively to change.

We can respond positively to the events, difficulties, stresses, problems, thoughts and emotions of life. As adults, we can also accept that doing this requires...

Practice!

Here's a quick-and-easy way to combine all of the **TRUE CALM** skills into a simple three-step process which you can use for the rest of your life to benefit, uplift yourself, and *THRIVE* with everything that happens around you and to you in your daily life.

Exercise

Pick a stress in your life, a problem or a difficulty, one that is current or upcoming for you. Now...

> A. Close your eyes and focus on that situation, picturing it, listening to your inner dialogue about it, and feeling how your body reacts.

B. Once you feel your body's response, produce *instant calm* to dissolve any potential survival or stress reactions.

C. From the state of calm, examine what it is about that situation you want LESS OF. Now change your perspective to what you want **MORE OF** in that same situation.

(With a partner: one person picks a stress while the other guides them through these three steps. The guide waits for their partner to signal when they have completed each step before proceeding to the next step. Then the partners can reverse roles.)

Did you end up with a goal, a positive focus you want **MORE OF**? That's the main purpose. This simple three-step process is called:

The THRIVING Response
(Figure 11.1)

You can use this simple three-step process to accomplish an array of valuable benefits. Keeping in mind that our evolution is now a matter of conscious choice, we need to know that in making the consistent effort to implement human *THRIVING*, we are literally programming our own nervous system. Each time there's stress, difficulty, problems or change, we **apply The THRIVING Response** and benefit. Why not? However, we quickly "learn" this new behavior pattern, and it becomes an automatic reaction to change. We don't need to think about it; we simply...

do it!

THE THRIVING RESPONSE

Step 1   CHANGE AWARENESS

A

Recognize when and how your body is signaling to get your attention.

B

Change your awareness to identify what is changing in the present.

Step 2   PRODUCE INSTANT CALM

A

Inhale deeply, energizing your Little Sun.

B

Exhale, releasing all muscles from forehead to feet.

C

Rest, hearing all external sounds with full Presence of Mind.

Step 3   THRIVE WITH YOUR AWARENESS OF CHANGE

A

Identify what you want LESS OF.

B

Change it to what you want MORE OF.

C

Stabilize your focus with the mental patterns of THRIVING.

Fig. 11.1

Let's summarize the practical functions of each aspect of **The *THRIVING* Response**.

Step 1. Change Awareness

The purpose of ***Change Awareness*** is to quickly become aware of change by recognizing our body talk, which usually appears in the form of stress. Next, we refocus our attention fully in the present, externally and internally, in order to identify what is changing. As discussed in Chapter Five, the first stage of ***Change Awareness*** we receive is akin to our "first impressions" that flash their insight, knowing and guidance into our attention ever so quickly. As we develop greater ***Presence of Mind***, we increase our ability to recognize these marvelous communications from our CENTER as they are breaking through into our consciousness. The more we spend time in the "perceiving" mode of ***Presence of Mind***, the more clear our conscious awareness is to "receive" the intuitive guidance from our CENTER on an ongoing, natural basis. This is how to benefit from the brilliance of our True SELF.

Remember: Although the change is already in process, our conscious mind is frequently the last part of us to know. "Stress" is designed to make us stop focusing on whatever we have been doing, and to make us immediately focus our attention in the present - so we can identify precisely what is changing - and respond positively.

Step 2. Produce Instant Calm

Immediately stopping the fight/flight emergency response effectively prevents the energy depleting wear-and-tear on our health. With *instant calm,* we're not forced to experience the world through the survival physiology of fight/flight, through the survival emotions of anger/fear, or through the singular dominating survival focus of what we want LESS OF, with its four mental patterns of a problem orientation.

Instead, we're mentally clear, calm, emotionally neutral and physically relaxed. We're energized with the inner joy of our *Life Energy*, not taxing our adrenal glands. In a state of calm "readiness," our whole attention capacity is free to identify and make good use of what is changing.

Step 3. *THRIVE* With Your Awareness Of Change

When we identify precisely what is changing, we can better **benefit** from change by using *The Big Lever* to move our focus into what we want **MORE OF** from what we want LESS OF. Then we can stabilize our focus in the motivation of *THRIVING* with the four key mental patterns of solutions regularly used by successful, creative, healthy and happy people. That's the deal!

It's now time to talk about...

***

THE MESSAGE

An adventure awaits you. Discovering your CENTER's message can be absolutely fascinating. Never limited to a single manner of expression, our CENTER nonetheless will often - and quite artfully - present its message in the form of our internal images, the feelings we have, and the dialogue going on within our minds. To get these valuable insights, we want to...

Recognize the actual content
of these internal sensations.

How do we do this? You already have the skills, for we access this inner material more easily in the state of **TRUE CALM**. To get the message, we simply focus in the present, but <u>internally</u>. We do this by looking inside for whatever images and pictures appear, while we are listening inside for whatever sounds and words are going on - which are usually talking about the images. And we sense inside for how we really feel about whatever is changing. **It is this combination of inner visual, inner auditory, and inner kinesthetic sensations that carries the message which "stress" is calling to our attention.**

The real secret to getting the message is to:

FEEL the sensory content!

How do the inner images and dialogue feel to you? Joyous? Scary? Happy? Upsetting? The feeling we have often provides its meaning to us. Frequently the images and pictures are of childhood scenes, with ourselves being small and helpless while some large adult is yelling at us. The actual words of our internal dialogue are usually critical, berating, blaming and discouraging to our confidence and our self esteem. We feel hurt.

Curiously, when we focus on these words, we can hear that the voices saying these damaging words are not even our own voice, but are the voices of our parents, a teacher, an older sibling or someone who was abusive and unkind to us. As adults, we need to know that if it's not OUR voice - and especially if it's not on OUR side, with OUR best interests at heart, helping us achieve

OUR most valued goals - then we can stop empowering it by giving it so much attention. Just like watering a plant helps it grow, we give "respect" by paying attention. Our attention empowers or energizes what we focus on. If something or someone doesn't deserve respect, then we don't honor it by continually focusing our attention in its direction.

We can reclaim our internal dialogue by challenging and confronting those voices with the present truth of who we are and what we want **MORE OF** as adults. When we bring these words and internal images to our consciousness, we can more easily examine them and change them into the supportive, encouraging, helpful, uplifting and loving words and images we want to have **MORE OF** inside our mind. After all, it's OUR mind. Whether we do it ourselves or with professional guidance,

This is how we uplift ourselves.

While most people are initially apprehensive or even afraid of focusing on or "facing" those inner skeletons, it is a liberating and confidence-producing thing to do, especially when we keep in mind how mechanical all this is. When we focus, consciously or unconsciously, on what we want LESS OF, we trigger fight/flight responses. When we focus, consciously or unconsciously, on what we want **MORE OF**, we trigger feelings of joy, confidence, excitement, pleasure, positive motivation and the warmth of love. It's simply a matter of directing our own focus. We want to identify and change the inner events into things we want **MORE OF**. We know we've been successful when we can then focus on them and **feel comfortable, confident or better**. That's the test.

What has prevented many people from accomplishing this release or "purging" of inner skeletons is the physical sensations of fear, anxiety and extreme discomfort. What are these? They are simply automatic fight/flight survival reactions which feel just like fear. The more these people tried to focus on, identify and deal with the inner voices and inner images they wanted LESS OF, the more intense were the sensations of fight/flight. Naturally, most folks would prefer to just leave it alone, since who knows how much more intense it might feel.

The good news is that with the skills for **TRUE CALM**, we can keep our calming mechanism turned on, our survival mechanism turned off, and finally identify just what was so fearful to see in the light of day! Often the internal events are simply remnants of our childhoods, but are still triggering fear-and-anger type expressions of fight/flight reactions. We need to update these internal events. One beneficial use of the state of **TRUE CALM** is to be able to focus fully in the present - internally - and dismantle these remnants in a relatively calm manner. (See Figure 11.2)

For example, a woman in her late fifties once had Crohn's disease, a condition where the colon is not absorbing water and nutrients, losing them through spasms of the lower intestines. While this can be lethal, the constant reality of diarrhea was most disrupting to her life; she needed to stay very close to a bathroom at all times. Working, socializing, driving and even leaving home were nearly impossible.

Through our work, we discovered that her life was completely immersed in simply "getting by." She was such a genuinely "giving" person that she was spending all her time, energy and focus supporting the other people in her life: her grown children, her boyfriend and her employer.

BENEFICIAL USES OF THE THRIVING RESPONSE

A

Successfully cope with rapid change.

B

Respond positively, effectively and with greater health to life's difficulties.

C

Use stress as a beneficial vehicle for continuous personal growth.

D

Transform personal stress and business problems into creative solutions and goal-achieving situations.

E

Help others respond more positively to the problems, events and changes in their own lives.

Fig. 11.2

Her boss would sometimes call her into his office just to have her hand him a piece of paper that was but two feet outside of his reach, and she would do it without complaining.

Basically, her CENTER was communicating to her, through the distress of Crohn's disease, that she had no reason to live because she was not living her own life, but everyone else's. The communication of her illness became clear. She had a choice: to reclaim her life or die.

She chose to live HER life, by discovering and choosing what she wanted **MORE OF** in every area of her life, and then by going for it and enjoying the results. Once she made her choice to *THRIVE*, all of her symptoms of Crohn's disease stopped and she became symptom free. At age fifty-six, she began enjoying her life more fully. She helped her boyfriend overcome his fears and marry her. She told her boss what she would do and not do. She began traveling and got involved with other activities that brought her joy.

She has remained free of symptoms and discomforts by finally nourishing herself and letting others meet their own needs. Her medical doctor concluded that he must have misdiagnosed her since he had never seen that illness remedied so dramatically. But when we pick up our inner phone and value the communication from our CENTER by acting on it, the ringing stops because it has served its purpose. With this imbalance corrected, the illness could then dissolve.

In fact, virtually every stress, every emotional problem, every medical condition, every illness, and every anxiety has this communication function to it. When we get the communication - and act on it with respect - the illness, stress or anxiety can dissolve because it has served its purpose. This understanding confirms what we all suspect at deeper levels within us: our minds, our bodies, our emotions, our energy, and our experience are all connected in purposeful, benevolent ways.

With this understanding and our desire to finally resolve our stressful problems, move on with our lives and benefit, we can quickly develop a more mature honesty with ourselves - in the form of a strong unwillingness to fool ourselves any longer. Our desire for the true message our CENTER is giving us generates a more open-minded curiosity, a curiosity that won't tolerate being restricted anymore by the old fears, anxieties and beliefs of survival's past dominance.

Generally, at this time, we are in the midst of an enormous and dramatic transition out of surviving - as individuals and as a species. Our CENTER is usually pointing the way for us to uplift ourselves into the *THRIVING* mode. It does this primarily by informing us of when we are stuck in the LESS OF patterns of survival. Unfortunately, this means stress... until we change. We can use **The Big Lever** to change our focus to what we want **MORE OF**. This is how we *THRIVE* with change...

WE change.

Sometimes the signal for change has been ignored for so long that the signals themselves have become health problems. Then we also need to remedy the effects of the signaling.

Born To *THRIVE*

With the struggles of survival nearly behind us, our species can now move into new realms, into the more benevolent, healthier and more fulfilling challenges. What will be the products, goods, services and technologies of a world fully focused on **THRIVING**? As we implement the **MORE OF** focus, we activate the neurological patterns that generate creavitity, innovation and "The Big Picture" of where we are going. As with all periods of innovation, fresh **THRIVING** products will probably trigger huge rewards. A great race! While we might not yet know the details of a **THRIVING** world, complete with technologies that replenish our natural resources so that all life can **THRIVE** on our beautiful planet, what we clearly do know is that...

BIG changes are on the way!

It is a very exciting time to be alive on our Planet EARTH. The rate of change has accelerated and will continue to do so because we are heading someplace. Always keep in mind: many otherwise decent folks will be reacting to change with our ancient fight/flight survival mechanism. This means fear, anger and sometimes violence. Like young children desperately clinging to <u>their</u> rubber ducky, they need to be soothed. We can calm them. We do so by cultivating calm inside ourselves and keeping our Little Sun beaming radiantly in our heart area. We stabilize ourselves and others in the **THRIVING** focus, concentrating on what we all want **MORE OF**.

We humans were not meant to exist on this beautiful planet in a perpetual state of fear and violence born of the desperations of survival. For it is time for our entire species to leave behind fear and anger as our primary motivations. Yet they are indeed useful for pointing out and avoiding the potholes of life.

However, as our guiding light, the important things we want **MORE OF** must occupy the role of our primary motivation.

We are meant to uplift ourselves into *THRIVING*, and we are meant to utilize the grander wisdom, fuller insight, greater understanding and creative brilliance of our CENTER to accomplish our highest life goals, our joys and our true desires through the art of *THRIVING* with change. But to do so we must respectfully stay tuned in with our CENTER, which is lovingly and benevolently guiding us to *THRIVE*.

It's very much like we have a path to travel on, our own individual path. When we depart from it, like radar, our CENTER prods us back by creating difficulties, stress and discomforts. The struggle to stay on our path is our adventure, our vehicle for learning, our process of growth. How wonderful that we have a path whose signs exist and guide us to *THRIVING*! The good news is that as a species, our time of being stuck in the struggles of survival are over.

We are now "supposed to" THRIVE.

The way of **TRUE CALM** involves going through our daily activities with our skeletal muscles relaxed when we're not using them; with our emotions calm and peaceful; with our Little Sun open and radiating its *Life Energy* throughout our body, with the mental clarity of *Presence of Mind* continuously receiving sensory information both externally and internally; and with our attention focused on what we want **MORE OF**, stabilized with the mental patterns of *THRIVING*. When something happens that takes us out of **TRUE CALM**, it can alert us to look for change. We can then use some manner of **The *THRIVING* Response** to identify the change and benefit from it by applying the **MORE OF** focus. (Figure 11.3)

THE THRIVING RESPONSE

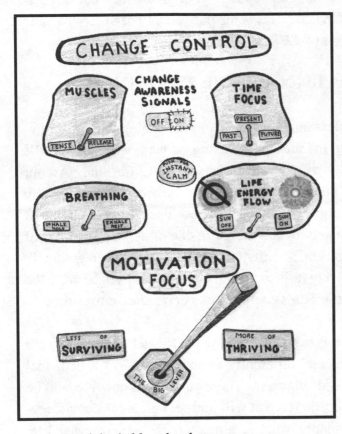

*Mechanically oper-
ating our four major
body systems together
in these specific ways
allows us to feel calm
instantly, especially
whenever our **Change
Awareness** signals
inform us that some-
thing is changing. We
can then more easily
focus in the MORE OF
direction of THRIVING.
In this practical way,
we can respond posi-
tively and with greater
health to life's changes,
effectively preventing
our survival reaction
from producing des-
tructive stress, restrict-
ing our perception, and
limiting our creative
responses to change.*

Surviving's blues has been our groove
To move beyond we now can choose
With change to **THRIVE**, our new pursuit
Focus, practice soon bear fruit.

For EARTH big changes, 'round the corner
Wondrous opportunities to garner
Who knows how much this world can flower
As we unleash our THRIVING POWER.

Fig. 11.3

249

Using the Little Sun to directly connect more and more fully with your essence, your CENTER, your core energy, is a wonderful adventure to embark upon. Your SELF is your deepest source of **TRUE CALM**. This is the pure energy of SELF-love and joy, the energy level of *THRIVING*.

What To Expect With THRIVING

Very pleasant surprises begin happening to us from living more calmly in the present, focusing on what we want **MORE OF**, and especially as a result of using our Little Sun. As our health-generating base of daily operating in the world, continually opening up the energy flow of our life develops a kind of engine of soothing, uplifting and joyous energy inside of us. Our feelings of confidence, self-esteem, security, joy and happiness keep gradually growing and positively influencing all areas of our lives because the opening of our Little Sun's energy flow is cumulative over time.

While this can happen very quickly, let's say that a year from now you will feel differently about yourself. You will feel better and better inside yourself. Three years from now you will be able to turn on your life force at will and feel great inside whenever you want, no matter what is going on in your external life. **While it may seem slow, it is steady and powerful.** And you will benefit greatly by practicing - remembering to turn on your Little Sun all through your daily activities, having it become more and more present for you. Its gifts can be increasingly enjoyed over a lifetime.

Most of all, you will notice how using **TRUE CALM** is a more joyous, more healthy and more satisfying way of living. Increasingly filling more areas of your life with what you want

MORE OF is the most fulfilling, energizing, uplifting and nurturing thing you can do both for yourself and for all those around you whom your life touches. You become an inspiration for others. You become a gift to yourself and to the world.

These qualities of **TRUE CALM** have been highly valued throughout history by other humans for the wisest of reasons. Now their regular use is of immense practical value. Discover for yourself by using these skills in your life. (See Figure 11.4)

Many extraordinary abilities can easily blossom as we cultivate this ancient state of "being" called **TRUE CALM**. You may be very pleasantly surprised. They are naturally occurring, built into us. Are you ready? With these skills, I hope you will enjoy the ride. As we change, let's finally uplift ourselves out of survival and...

ACTIVATE HUMAN THRIVING!

KEY GOAL

VIGOROUSLY
APPLY
the THRIVING Response
and uplift yourself
continuously

Fig. 11.4

NOTES

Introduction
1.   Bach, Richard, Illusions. The Adventures of a Reluctant Messiah, Dell Publishing, New York, 1977.

Chapter 1
1.   Shah, Idries, The Way of the Sufi, Penguin Books, London, 1974.

2.   Zaichkowsky, L. & Kamen, R., Biofeedback and meditation: Effects on muscle tension and locus of control. *Perceptual & Motor Skills*, 45:955-58, 1978.

Morse, D.L., Martin, J.S., Furst, M.L. et al. Physiological and subjective evaluation of meditation, hypnosis relaxation. *Psychosomatic Medicine*, 39:304-24, 1977.

Haynes, S., Mosley, D. & McGowan, W. Relaxation training and biofeedback in the reduction of frontalis muscle tension, *Psychophysiology*, 12:547-52,1975.

Credidio, S.G., Comparative effectiveness of patterned biofeedback vs. meditation training on EMG and skin temperature changes. *Behavior Research & Therapy*,20:233-41, 1982.

3.   Pollard, G. & Ashton, R., Heart rate decrease: A comparison of feedback modalities and biofeedback with other procedures. *Biological Psychology*, 14:245-57, 1982.

Throll, D., Transcendental Meditation and Progressive Relaxation: Their physiological effects, *Journal of Clinical Psychology*, 37:776-81,1982.

Lang, R., Dehob, K., Meurer, K. et al, Sympathetic activity and TM. *Journal of Neural Transmission*, 44:117-35,1979.

Glueck, B. & Stroebel, C., Biofeedback as meditation in the treatment of psychiatric illness, *Comprehensive Psychiatry*, 16:303-21,1975.

Wallace, R.K., Benson, H. The physiology of meditation. *Scientific American*, 226,84-9O,1972.

Wallace, R.K., Benson, H.; Wilson, A.F. A wakeful hypometabolic physiologic state, *American Journal of Physiology*, 221,795-799,1971.

Wallace, R.K., Physiological effects of Transcendental Meditation. *Science*, 167:1751-54, 1970.

4.   Wallace, R.K., Silver, J., and Mills, P. et al. Systolic blood pressure and long-term practice of the Transcendental Meditation and TM-sidhi program: Effects of TM on systolic blood pressure. *Psychosomatic Medicine*, 45:41-46, 1983.

Bagga O. and Ghandi, A. A comparative study of the effect of Transcendental Meditation and Shavasana practice on the cardiovascular system, *Indian Heart Journal*, 35:39-45,1983.

Hafner, R., Psychological treatment of essential hypertension: A controlled comparison of meditation and meditation plus biofeedback. *Biofeedback and Self-Regulation*, 7:305-16,1982.

Seer, P., & Raeburn, J., Meditation training and essential hypertension: A methodological study. *Journal of Behavioral Medicine*, 3:59-70, 1980.

Surwit, R., Shapiro, D., Good, M. et al, Comparison of cardiovascular biofeedback, neuromuscular biofeedback, and meditation in the treatment of borderline essential hypertension, *Journal of Consulting & Clinical Psychology*, 46:252-63, 1978.

Blackwell, B., Bloomfield, S., Gartside, P. et al, Transcendental Meditation in hypertension: Individual response patterns, *Lancet*, 1:223-36, 1976.

Stone, R., & DeLeo, J., Psychotherapeutic control of hypertension, *New England of Medicine*, 2:80-4, 1976.

Patel, C., & North, W., Randomized control trial of yoga and biofeedback in management of hypertension, *Lancet*, 2:93-95,1975.

Benson, H., Rosner, B., & Marzetta, B., et al. Decreased blood pressure in untreated borderline hypertensive subjects who regularly elicited the relaxation response, *Clinical Research*, 22:262,1974.

Benson, H., et al. Decreased systolic blood pressure through operant conditioning techniques in patients with essential hypertension, *Science*, 173:740-42,1971.

Benson, H., & Wallace, R., Decreased blood pressure in hypertensive subjects who practiced meditation, *Circulation*, 46:1:130,1972.

Deabler, H., Fidel, E., Dillenkoffer, R., et al. The use of relaxation and hypnosis in lowering high blood pressure, *American Journal of Clinical Hypnosis*, 16:75-83,1973.

5.   Glueck, B., & Stroebel, C., Psychophysiologial correlates of meditation: EEG changes during meditation. In *Meditation: Classic & Contemporary Perspectives*, Shapiro, D.H., & Walsh, R. (eds.), Aldine, 1984.

Glueck, B. & Stroebel, C., Biofeedback as meditation in the treatment of psychiatric illness, *Comprehensive Psychiatry*, 16:303-21,1975.

Wallace, R.K., Benson, H.; Wilson, A.F. A wakeful hypometabolic physiologic state, *American Journal of Physiology*, 221,795-799,1971.

Wallace, R.K., Physiological effects of Transcendental Meditation. *Science*, 167:1751-54, 1970.

Taneli, B., & Krahne, W. EEG changes of Transcendental Meditation practitioners, *Advances in Biological Psychiatry*, 16:41-71,1987.

Pelletier, K., & Peper, E. Alpha EEG feeback as a means for pain control, *Journal of Clinical & Experimental Hypnosis*, 25:361-71,1977.

Banquet, J.P. EEG and meditation, *Electroencephalography & Clinical Neurophysiology*, 33:454,1972.

Banquet, J.P. Spectral analysis of the EEG in meditation, *Electroencephalography & Clinical Neurophysiology*, 35:143-51,1973.

6.   Zaichkowsky, L. & Kamen, R., Biofeedback and meditation: Effects

on muscle tension and locus of control. *Perceptual & Motor Skills*, 45:955-58, 1978.

Morse, D.L., Martin, J.S., Furst, M.L. et al. Physiological and subjective evaluation of meditation, hypnosis relaxation. *Psychosomatic Medicine*, 39:304-24, 1977.

Wallace, R.K.; Benson, H.; Wilson, A.F.; Garrett, M.D. Decreased blood lactate during Transcendental Meditation. *Federation Proceedings*, 3O:376,1971.

Haynes, S., Mosley, D. & McGowan, W. Relaxation training and biofeedback in the reduction of frontalis muscle tension, *Psychophysiology*, 12:547-52,1975.

Credidio, S.G., Comparative effectiveness of patterned biofeedback vs. meditation training on EMG and skin temperature changes. *Behavior Research & Therapy*,20:233-41, 1982.

Wallace, R.K., Benson, H.; Wilson, A.F. A wakeful hypometabolic physiologic state, *American Journal of Physiology*, 221,795-799,1971.

Wallace, R.K., Physiological effects of Transcendental Meditation. *Science*, 167:1751-54, 1970.

Orme-Johnson, D.W. Autonomic stability and Transcendental Meditation, *Psychosomatic Medicine*, 35:341-49,1973.

Wallace, R.K.; Benson, H.; Wilson, A.F.; Garrett, M.D. Decreased blood lactate during Transcendental Meditation. *Federation Proceedings*, 3O:376,1971.

7.   Cannon, W.B., The Wisdom of the Body. W.W. Norton & Co., New York, 1932.

Cannon, W.B., Bodily Changes in Pain, Hunger, Fear and Rage: An Account of Recent Research into the Function of Emotional Excitement. D. Appleton & Co., New York, London, 2nd edition, 1929.

8.   American Institute of Stress, Yonkers, New York.

9.   Fifth International Montreux Congress on Stress, 1993.

10.   Basmajian, J.V. Control and training of individual motor units, *Science*, 141:440-41, 1963.

Basmajian, J.V. Conscious control of single nerve cells, *New Scientist*, Dec. 12, 1966.

Chapter 2

1.   Shah, Idries. The Dermis Probe, The Octagon Press, London, 1970, 1980.

Chapter 3

1.   Shah, Idries. The Dermis Probe, The Octagon Press, London, 1970, 1980.

2.   Cannon, W.B., The Wisdom of the Body. W.W. Norton & Co., New York, 1932.

Cannon, W.B., <u>Bodily Changes in Pain, Hunger, Fear and Rage: An Account of Recent Research into the Function of Emotional Excitement</u>. D. Appleton & Co., New York, London, 2nd edition, 1929.

3. Shapiro, Barry A. <u>Clinical Application of Blood Gases</u>. Year Book Medical Publishers, Inc., Chicago, 1973.

4. Lum, L.C. The Syndrome of Chronic Hyperventilation. *Modern Trends in Psychosomatic Medicine*, Volume 3, London, Butterworth, Appleton-Century Crofts, New York, 1976.

Ayman, D.; Goldshine, A. The breath-holding test - a simple standard stimulus of blood pressure. *Archives of Internal Medicine*, 63:899-906, 1939.

Perris, E.; Engel, G.; Stevens, C.; Webb, J. voluntary breathholding III. The relation of the maximum time of breathholding to the oxygen and carbon dioxide tensions of arterial blood, with a note on its clinical and physiological significance. *Journal of Clinical Investigation*, Vol.25:734-743, 1946.

5. Bolton, B.; Carmichael, E.; Sturrup, G. Vasoconstriction following respiratory inspiration. *Journal of Physiology*, London 86:83, 1936. In Sharpey-Shafer, E.P. Effects of respiratory acts on the circulation. <u>Handbook of Physiology</u>, Vol. 3(2), Circulation, 1975-1886, 1964, American Physiological Society, Washington, D.C.

Shapiro, Barry A. <u>Clinical Application of Blood Gases</u>. Year Book Medical Publishers, Inc., Chicago, 1973.

6. Haldane, J.S. Respiration. New Haven: Yale University Press, 1922. In Richards, D. circulatory effects of hyperventilation and hypoventilation. <u>Handbook of Physiology</u>, Vol. 3(2), Circulation, 1975-1886, 1964, American Physiological Society, Washington, D.C.

Engel, G.; Ferris, E.; Logan, M. Hyperventilation: Clinical symptomatology. *Annals of Internal Medicine*, 27,683-704,1947.

7. Shapiro, Barry A. <u>Clinical Application of Blood Gases</u>. Year Book Medical Publishers, Inc., Chicago, 1973.

Engel, G.; Ferris, E.; Logan, M. Hyperventilation: Clinical symptomatology. *Annals of Internal Medicine*, 27,683-704,1947.

8. Engel, G.; Ferris, E.; Logan, M. Hyperventilation: Clinical symptomatology. *Annals of Internal Medicine*, 27,683-704,1947.

Richards, D. circulatory effects of hyperventilation and hypoventilation. <u>Handbook of Physiology</u>, Vol. 3(2), Circulation, 1975-1886, 1964, American Physiological Society, Washington, D.C.

9. Cooper, Kenneth H. <u>The New Aerobics</u>. New York, Bantam Books, 1970.

Cooper, Kenneth H. <u>Running Without Fear</u>. New York, Bantam Books, 1985.

Fixx, James F. <u>The Complete Book Of Running</u>. Random House, New York, 977.

10. Wallace, R.K.; Benson, H. The physiology of meditation. *Scientific American*, 226,84-90,1972.

Benson, H. The Mind/Body Effect. New York: Simon & Schuster, 1979.

Benson, H. Beyond The Relaxation Response. New York: Times Books, 1984.

11.   Benson, H.; Dryer, T.; Hartley, L.H. Decreased oxygen consumption during exercise with elicitation of the Relaxation Response. *Journal of Human Stress*, 4, 38-42, 1978.

Wallace, R.K.; Benson, H.; Wilson, A.F. A wakeful hypometabolic physiologic state. *American Journal of Physiology*, 221,795-799, 1971.

Benson, H. The Relaxation Response. New York, William Morrow, 1975.

Benson, H; Beary, J.F.; Carol, M.P. The Relaxation Response, *Psychiatry*, 37, 37-46, 1974.

12.   Jacobson, E. Progressive Relaxation. Chicago: University of Chicago Press, 1936.

Wallace, R.K.; Benson, H.; Wilson, A.F.; Garrett, M.D. Decreased blood lactate during Transcendental Meditation. *Federation Proceedings*, 3O:376,1971.

13.   Benson, H et al. Decreased blood pressure in borderline hypertensive subjects who practiced meditation. *Journal of Chronic Diseases*, 27, 163-169, 1974.

Benson, H. Systemic hypertension and the Relaxation Response. *New England Journal of Medicine*, 296, 1152-1156, 1977.

14.   Barach, A. Breathing exercises in pulmonary emphysema and allied chronic respiratory disease. *Archives of Physical Medicine*, 36:55 (January), 1954.

Barach, A.; Beck, G. The ventilatory effects of the head down position in pulmonary emphysema. *American Journal of Medicine*, 16:55 (January), 1954.

Miller, W. A physiologic evaluation of the effects of diaphyagmatic breathing training in patients with chronic emphysema. *American Journal of Medicine*, 17:471 (October), 1954.

Plum, F. Neurological integration of behavioral and metabolic control of breathing. In Breathing: Hering Breuer Centenary Symposium, Ruth Porter (Ed.), J. & A. Churchill, London, 197O.

Cherniack, R.M.; Cherniack, L.; Naimark, A. Respiration In Health And Disease. W.B. Saunders Co., Philadelphia, London, Toronto, 1972.

Mills, J.N. *Journal of Physiology*, London, 1O4,1945. In Breathing: Hering Breuer Centenary Symposium, Ruth Porter (Ed.), J. & A. Churchill, London, 197O.

Dudley, D.L.; Martin, C.J.; Holmes, T.H. *Psychosomatic Medicine*, 26:645-66O, 1964. In Plum, F. Neurological integration of behavioral and metabolic control of breathing. In Breathing: Hering Breuer Centenary Symposium, Ruth Porter (Ed.), J. & A. Churchill, London, 197O.

15.   Shapiro, Barry A. Clinical Application of Blood Gases. Year Book Medical Publishers, Inc., Chicago, 1973.
16.   Brown, Barbara. New Mind, New Body: Biofeedback. New York, Harper & Row, 1974.

Brown, Barbara. Stress And The Art Of Biofeedback. Harper & Row, New York, 1977.
17.   Benson, H.; Klemchuk, H.P.; Graham, J.R.; The usefulness of the relaxation response in the therapy of headache. Headache, 14, 49-52, 1974.

Naranjo, C.; Ornstein, R.E. On the Psychology of Meditation. New York, Viking Press, 1971.

Benson, H. et al. Treatment of anxiety: A comparison of the usefulness of self hypnosis and a meditational relaxation technique. Psychotherapy and Psychosomatics, 3O, 229-242, 1978.

Basmajian, John V. Biofeedback: Principals And Practice For Clinicians. Second Edition, Williams & Wilkins, 1983.

Chapter Four

1.   Shah, Idries. The Dermis Probe, The Octagon Press, London, 1970, 1980.
2.   Jacobson, E. Progressive Relaxation, Chicago, University of Chicago Press, 1936.
3.   Isaac, Ramon, D.O. Personal communication,1992.

Chapter Five

1.   Suzuki, Shunryu. Zen Mind, Beginner's Mind, Weatherhill, New York & Tokyo,1970.
2.   Narranjo, C. Present-centeredness: technique, prescription, and ideal. in Gestalt therapy now: theory, techniques, applications. (Eds.) Joen Fagan and Irma Lee Shepherd,Palo Alto,Calif.,Sciences and Behavior Books,1970.
3.   Miller, G. The magic number seven, plus Or minus two: Some limits on our capacity for processing information, Psychological Review, 63:81-97, 1956.

Chapter Six

1.   Shah, Idries. The Dermis Probe, The Octagon Press, London, 1970, 1980.
2.   Peters, Ron, M.D. Personal communication,1986.
3.   Gendlin, Eugene T. Focusing, Bantam Books, Inc., New York,1981.

Chapter Seven

1.   Shah, Idries. The Dermis Probe, The Octagon Press, London, 1970, 1980.
2.   Davidson, John. The Secret of the Creative Vacuum, C.W. Daniel Company Limited, England, 1989.

3.   Lu, James. Personal communication, 1993.
4.   Darras, Jean-Claude, M.D. and De Vernejoul, P., M.D. Presented at the World Research Foundation Congress on Bio-Energetic Medicine, 1986.
5.   Nordenstrom, B.E., Impact of biologically closed electric circuits (BCEC) on structure and function, *Integr. Physiol. Behav. Sci.*, 27, 285-303, 1992.

      Rosch, P.J., Future directions in psychoneuroimmunology: psycho-electroneuroimmunology?, in <u>Stress, the Immune System and Psychiatry</u>, Leonard, B., Miller, K., Eds., John Wiley & Sons, London, 1995 (in press).

      Belehradek, M., Domenge, C., Luboinski, B., Orlowski, S., Belehradek, J. and Mir, L.M., Electrotherapy, a new antitumor treatment. First clinical phase I-II trial, *Cancer*, 72,3694-700, 1993.

      Salford, L.G., Persson, B.R., Brun, A., Ceberg, C.P., Knogstad,P.C., and Mir, L.M., A new brain tumor therapy conbining bleomycin with in vivo electropermeabilization, *Biochem Biophys Res Commun*, 194, 938-43, 1993.

      Becker, Robert O., M.D. and Seldon, Gary. <u>The Body Electric</u>: <u>Electromagnetism and the Foundation of Life</u>, William Morrow & Co., Inc., 1985.

      Green, E.E., Parks, Peter A., Guyer, Paul, M., Fahrion, Steven L., Coyne, Lolafaye. Anomalous electrostatic phenomena in exceptional subjects, *Subtle Energies*, Volume 2, Number 3.
6.   Suzuki, Shunryu. <u>Zen Mind, Beginner's Mind</u>, Weatherhill, New York & Tokyo,1970.
7.   Jonathan. Personal communication, 1989.
8.   Brown, Barbara B. Supermind: <u>The Ultimate Energy</u>, Bantam Books, New York, 198O.
9.   ibid.

Chapter Eight
1.   Shah, Idries. <u>The Dermis Probe</u>, The Octagon Press, London, 1970, 1980.
2.   Gerber, Richard, M.D. <u>Vibrational Medicine</u>: New Choices For Healing Ourselves, Bear & Company, Sante Fe, New Mexico, 1988.
3.   Selye, H. <u>The Stress Of Life</u>, McGraw-Hill Book Co., New York, 1956, 1976 (Revised Edition).
4.   Ibid.
5.   Ibid.

Chapter Nine
1.   Shah, Idries. <u>The Dermis Probe</u>, The Octagon Press, London, 1970, 1980.
2.   Ornstein, R.; Sobel, D. <u>The Healing Brain</u>. Touchstone Books, Simon & Schuster, Inc., New York, 1987.

      Ornstein, Robert and Thompson, Richard F. <u>The Amazing Brain</u>,

Houghton Mifflin Company, Boston, 1994.

3.   ibid.
4.   ibid.
5.   ibid.
6.   ibid.
7.   ibid.
8.   ibid.
9.   Solomon, G.F. Psychoneuroimmunology: Interactions between central nervous system and immune system, *Journal of Neuroscience Research*, 18:1-9 (1987).

Solomon, G.F. Emotional and personality factors in the onset and course of autoimmune disease, particularly rheumatoid arthritis. In Ader R. (ed): Psychoneuroimmunology. New York: Academic Press, pp159-179.

Dixon, F.J.; Feldman, J,; Vasquez, J.; Experimental glomerulonephritis. *Journal of Experimental Medicine*, 113:899, 1961.

Hamburg, D.A., Plasma and urinary corticosteroid levels in naturally occurring psychological stresses. *Res Publ Assoc Res Nerv Ment Dis* 40:406, 1962.

Pelletier, Kenneth R., Mind as Healer, Mind as Slayer. New York, Delta, 1977.

Pelletier, Kenneth R., Holistic Medicine: From Stress to Optimal Health. Nwe York: Delta, 1979.

Antonovsky, Aaron. Health, Stress and Coping. San Francisco: Jossey-Bass, 1979.

Borysenko, Joan. Minding the Body, Mending the Mind, Bantam Books, Toronto, 1987.

Kabat-Zinn, Jon. Full Catastrophe Living, Dell Publishing, New York, 1990.

Siegel, Bernie S. Love, Medicine & Miracles, Harper & Row, New York, 1986.

10.   Grinder, John and Bandler, Richard, NEURO-LINGUISTIC PROGRAMMING.
11.   ibid.
12.   Bennett, Cleaves, M.D. Control Your High Blood Pressure Without Drugs, Doubleday,1984.

Chapter Ten
1.   Saadi in: Shah, Idries, The Way of the Sufi, Penguin Books, London, 1974.

Chapter Eleven
1.   Shah, Idries. The Dermis Probe, The Octagon Press, London, 1970, 1980.